Metal Thread Embroidery

Metal Thread Embroidery

Barbara Dawson

B. T. Batsford Limited

© Barbara Dawson 1968 and 1976
First published 1968
New edition 1976

Printed in Great Britain by
Morrison & Gibb, Edinburgh
for the Publishers
B T Batsford Limited
4 Fitzhardinge Street London W1H 0AH

ISBN 0 7134 3144 X

Contents

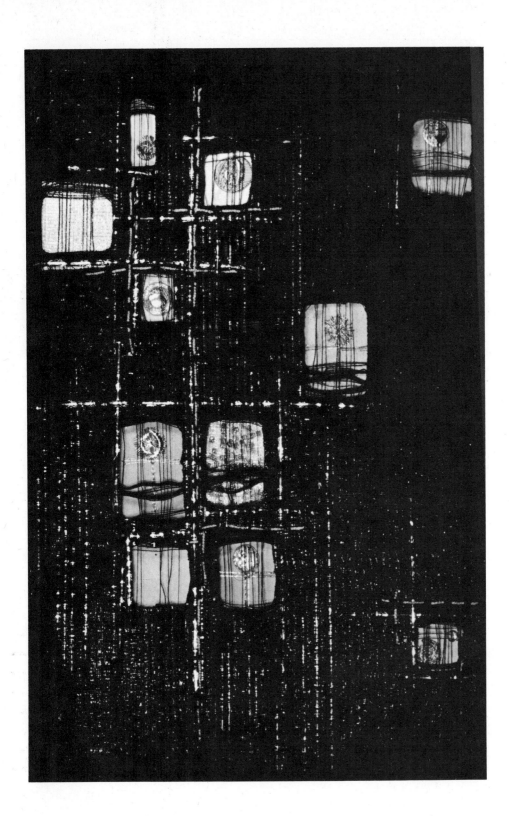

Night The entire surface is covered with a fine wool black cloth which is woven with light gold raffia. The positions of the gold work areas were traced off, marked and cut out of the black to allow the gold to show through. This immediately shows the design of square windows, 'which are then linked by a very restrained use of thread in chenille and raffia. These two threads are not only a foil for each other in texture, but also repeat in line and the colour of the solid shapes

Acknowledgment

I would like to thank the Principal of Goldsmiths College, School of Art, and particularly Constance Howard, Head of Department of Embroidery and Textiles, and the staff and students, for permission to include examples of my students' work and for the generous co-operation in the exchange of ideas, including those on photography.

I would also thank John Hunnex of the Graphic Department, School of Art, whose inspired printing improved many of my own inexpert photographs and who overcame many difficulties with his own professional photographs and the four colour plates.

For permission to use works outside the School of Art, I am grateful to Michael Greater of Goldsmiths College for examples of his students' work; Miss M. M. Phelps, Goldsmiths College Administration, for figure 44 from the College Report; The Trustees of the British Museum for reproduction of the Rembrandt drawings, 135–41; The Provost of Chelmsford Cathedral to include photographs of the cope, 154–69; The Vicar of St Mary's Church, North Mymms for the brass rubbing, 142; The Crafts Council of Great Britain to show the cope, 152; The County of Warwick School Loan Collection of the Warwick Museum for the letter composition, 26–30; The Embroiderers Guild to reproduce parts of an article, from their Guild Journal, and to Frederick Brittain, D. Litt, Fellow of Jesus College, Cambridge for his kind help with the proofs.

B.D.   Barnet 1968, 1976

Introduction

Metal thread embroidery has acquired a new place today because of the opportunities it gives for the interpretation of individual design. The subtleties of the threads are more varied than in any other type of embroidery, and express a simple foundation design as superbly as a more intricate one.

The metal threads available vary from pure gold, silver and alloys to synthetic imitations. Platinum and uranium may have superseded gold as the most precious metal, but the lustre and beauty of the latter has not changed.

The imagination is involuntarily drawn from the pomp of impressive regalia to the aesthetic quality of the golden thread which gives a feeling of inspiring light and brightness associated with dreams of rare and treasured gifts, the magnanimity of kings, the magic of early civilizations, the richness of ceremony, and the poetry of mysticism and religion.

The metal character of goldwork is another difference from any other type of embroidery, being akin to jewellery and even sculpture, because the surface appears faceted as the light catches different angles of the thread which padding accentuates. Each thread takes on a character of its own, and each stitch an individual importance in the setting, or support, of the design. All hand embroidery should reflect the most telling use of thread and stitch, together with a scale of work suited to design, background, thread and stitch. Goldwork is a perfect medium to be exploited in this way; over-fine work is lost and detail wasted, whilst coarse work does not contain sufficient interest to maintain repeated viewing. The work is often considered slow, but as it progresses it is possible to give thought to the building of the design, and to the value of each technique, such as whether rows of repetitive work, so often synonymous with a mechanical outlook, contribute more than an area of appliqué, and to avoid a smart work with a veneer of taste.

In explaining the methods applied to goldwork, a start is made at the core of metal thread embroidery, these methods can then be adapted to other metal threads. Threads for goldwork can be put into three categories. First of all japanese gold which is in a class of its own as it is pure gold and has a most magnificent and lasting colour, it requires the most care to work, is the most expensive, yet fairly easy to obtain. Second and third are Admiralty quality threads and purls which have a high proportion of gold, and are therefore less expensive than japanese gold. The threads may be couched, and the purls sewn in various ways. A certain amount of care in selection is of course necessary.

Many factors make it worthwhile to buy the best threads available. These in goldwork are often the most expensive, as they have the greatest gold content. The cheaper quality tends to discolour fairly quickly, whilst silver turns black in time, and thus produces disappointing results. The untarnishable aluminium threads which often replace silver tend to appear grey and lack brilliance. Whereas a certain amount of discolouration takes place in any threads that are not pure gold, the better quality produces wonderful gradations of red brown and yellow black.

These gradations are lacking in the synthetic threads because although they are available in colours and do not tarnish, the amount of shine seems constant, giving an unvarying glitter which does not have the softness or warmth of gold. The synthetic threads can be used very successfully for filling out a design, and acting as a supporting role where there is a preponderance of good quality thread. The richness is achieved by the real gold, the synthetic thread prevents the cost being excessive.

Important and bold results are obtained in many of the braids and novelty threads which are produced and are readily obtainable. These are easy to use though somewhat limited in scope and tend to

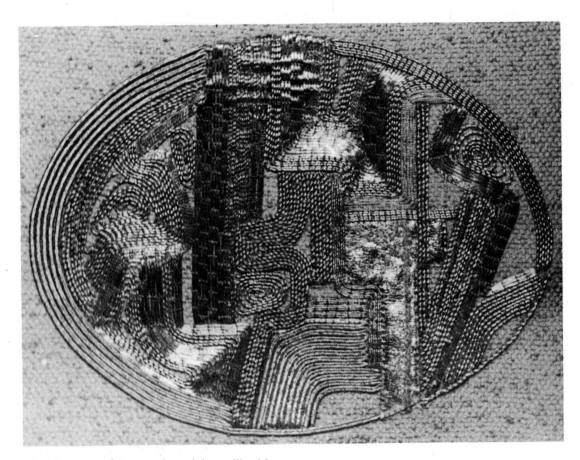

1 Design on a soft curry coloured dress silk with a
bouclé texture, worked in a wide variety of couched
metal threads which catch the light, giving a
faceted appearance   *Lynn Jones*

give the work a sparkling and passing triviality if
not used with convincing élan. A successful use of
synthetic threads is to give decorative effects worked
by the machine. These are valuable design experiments but, as only few threads are suitable, the results tend to be thin. This defect can be overcome
by working in a richer scale with handwork, either
in metal or other embroidery threads of good
quality, and sympathetic or striking colour.

The worker is also affected by the thrill of using
costly threads, which act as such a source of
stimulus, and an average worker can become out-
standing, aiming for a thoughtful result, rather

than a cheap, quick, tawdry, phantasy of momen-
tary interest.

Much of the success of goldwork lies in the
manipulation of the threads, and this skill requires
time. This, together with the time and effort given
to the design, as well as the preliminary work of
framing up, seems wasted if the work is marred by
tarnishing through having used poor materials.
This applies equally to the ground materials and to
the introduction of other threads.

Time being such a precious commodity the
simplest, most straight forward, yet essential
methods are explained. Once the basic essentials

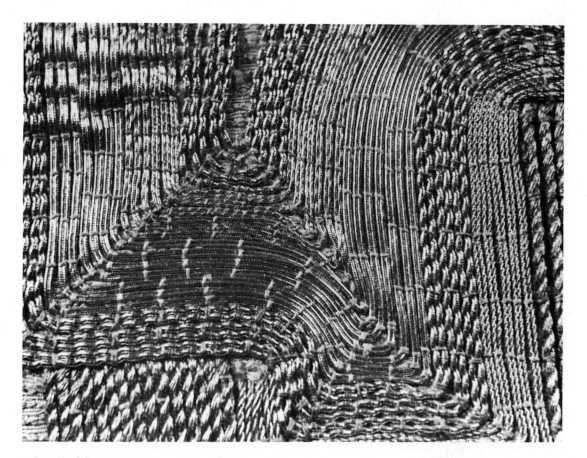

2 Detail of threads showing, right to centre: cord, twist, crinkle, smooth passing, wavy passing, japanese gold, crinkle at centre. This is an example of rows of hand couched threads having more value than repetitive rows of machining as the textures and turns would hardly be manageable by machine. Note double stitch at corners

are understood, many personally successful ways of working can be evolved.

To spend a vast amount of time on preliminaries seems unnecessary when experimenting or when a worker is exploring an unknown medium. An aptitude for this work may develop easily, but discouragement may result if elaborate preparations are not rewarded with success. On the other hand, the simple preparations must be accurate.

Several books give detailed information on the practical side of embroidery and supply diagrams which, however clear, necessarily exaggerate the proportions, and so sometimes confuse a beginner. As the workers' experience and confidence expands these books are invaluable for reference. Through the photographs in this book it is the intention of the author to give a true picture of the working methods and it is hoped they will be more readily understood than isolated diagrams unrelated to design and which, because time is needed to select the relevant parts, often delay the start of an embroidery. Preparations kept to a minimum give more time for developing embroidery and design, and prevent a tendency to maul and mutilate the threads in an attempt merely to be original.

3–6 Groups of flat and padded shapes, some with string on felt, others with felt or string only, on a soft green slubbed silk ground. Couched metal threads and purls are used with silk and crewel wool french knots and laid lines

Pauline Watson

The threads are obtainable from several suppliers. Some of the threads are still craftsman-made or made by hand, and probably by only one manufacturer. The metal is drawn out in much the same way as the wire-drawers of the eleventh and twelfth centuries, coiled for purl, or wound round a core for couching thread.

A natural reluctance to catalogue what is such an individual commodity is understandable as it is not always possible to guarantee an exactly repeated order, but this is a unique part of the work and should be accepted as a challenge to the verve of the worker to take what is available and turn it to good account.

7 Detail at right; check purl covers string between couched gold. Left; check purl chips used as a filling and a seeding, note two angles of using purl chips. Cords, crinkle and imitation jap, are used with silk french knots and straight stitches to form a flower pattern and outline   *Penny Wallington*

When an awkwardly shaped piece of precious material has great appeal there is no better way to preserve it than as part of a ground. See also figures 26, 35 and 186.

Opposite

8 'The Seasons' panel on a parti-coloured background of yellow, pink and brown with experimental methods in as great variety as possible. Shows a way of preserving small pieces of precious material   *Barbara Dawson*

This attitude also applies to discrepancies that may occur in the work. Embroidery should not necessarily be unpicked, as the thread is then wasted and the ground material weakened. Instead any unsatisfactory work should be made a feature of the design by working it over with silk or another type of metal thread, such as adding an extra thread to rows of gold couching which become too openly spaced, or extra couching stitches in a pattern form to jap gold that shows the core.

10 An achievement very regularly worked, in evenly cut purl and evenly worked long and short stitches giving a flat stamped out appearance by closely working from a painted design, and giving a somewhat static result which is occasionally required for badges and regalia. Note the use of long and short in purl for the mantling. The slanting silk long and short for the lion rampant is a typical method of working heraldic beasts and lettering
Barbara Dawson

9 Detail of a head in jap gold showing invisibility of bricked couching which can however be seen top right. Silk couching and purls mark features and also cover any tendency for the orange core of the jap to show up and also fills any spaces in couching, preventing a hard mechanical appearance. Jewels and sequins in the coronet are set in purls which mark out the earrings as well
Dorothy Burchmore

This may seem to be cheating by some standards, but in this way standardisation is avoided, and many new and exciting results are developed.

The standard idea of a sampler should be reconsidered, as a first piece of work is often very successful, and need not be thought of as a throwaway. Working with the unknown often produces more lively work than when calculated results are sought after. A closely followed paper and paint

design can rarely make a marvellous embroidery for it tends to look like imitation paper and paint, a possible exception being regalia or heraldic charges for commercial requirements.

In any case, preconceived ideas often present the difficulty of not being successful in reality, yet when working with the nature of the threads an adaptable partnership can be established with the work.

To begin any embroidery with areas of laborious technique seems a sterile approach, but the choice of shape, repeated in design form, i.e. a plan or pattern, may have a variety of methods held together by the thread, colour and shape, and this becomes a foundation design.

Equipment and Materials

Square frame consisting of crossbars running horizontally, slatted with arms running vertically.

Ring frame 8 to 9 in. A smaller size makes working conditions too cramped. If larger it is difficult to maintain an evenly taut tension of the fabric in the frame.

Two thimbles One for the third finger of each hand.

Needles Crewel needles have a long narrow eye making a smooth needle. They are easy to thread and suitable for all sewing including framing up, mounting and making up.

Crewel needles

    no. 5   for strong thread and framing up

    no. 8   for tacking appliqué and transferring design and some couching

    no. 10 for use with purls.

Chenille needles are a large, strong needle having a large eye and a sharp point similar to a stiletto

    no. 18 for taking down ends of metal threads.

Packing needle for string.

Scissors Nail scissors are best for cutting the wire of metal threads but not with curved blades. The blades are tough, short, strong and sharp to cut accurately at a right angle to the thread without waste.

Embroidery scissors for usual threads

Cutting-out scissors

Paper scissors.

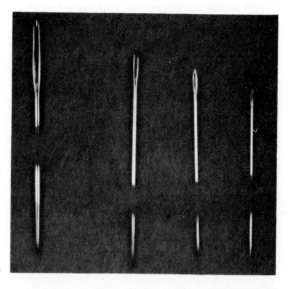

11 Note long narrow smooth eye of needle and sharp point from left to right

Stiletto Preferably with a flat sided handle.

Steel pins

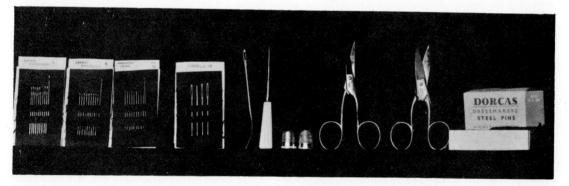

12 Note short thick blades of scissors for cutting metal thread

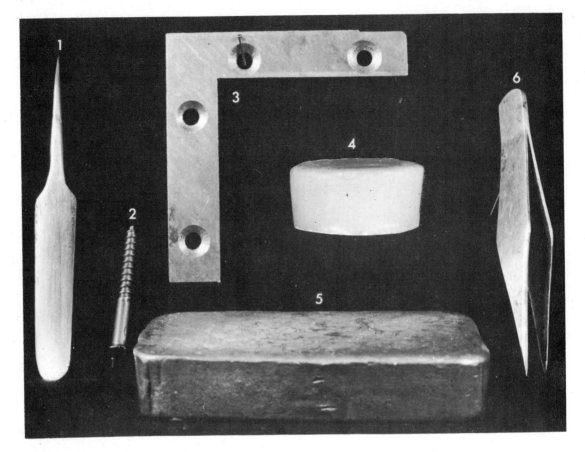

13 1 Mellore
2 Screw for crimping plate
3 Metal right angle bracket
4 Beeswax
5 Lead weight
6 Burling irons

Burling irons or *tweezers* may be used to avoid unnecessary handling of purls and jewels when planning and moving positions.

Melor or awl Similar to a flat stiletto, not now manufactured, but found in junk shops; or similar instrument is found in old-fashioned manicure sets, may be used for turning metal thread at angles.

Cutting board Baize, velvet or felt glued on to a piece of board which is used as a firm base for cutting purl. See figures 115 and 116.

Felt Matched to the thread to be used: such as deep yellow for gold, and grey for silver.

String Strong for use in framing up and for some padding in the embroidery, with a finer one for variation.

If obtainable, yellow macramé string is ideal though the manufacture is now discontinued. Some yellow twines are on the market but these seem to be of paper construction and are too flimsy to support the metal thread when used as a padding.

To obtain a colour, dip the string in ink to match the thread – yellow for gold – before working to avoid string showing in the embroidery.

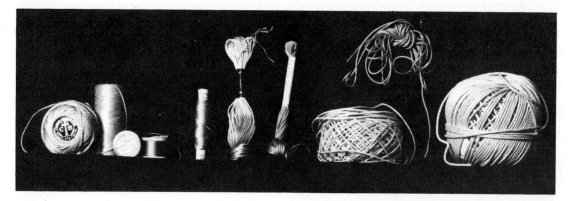

14 From left to right: thick thread for framing up. Maltese silk, perivale, stranded cotton, filoselle for other processes. String for framing up and padding. Macramé string in background

Threads for sewing Maltese silk for couching metal threads. Three colours are available; two shades of yellow for gold, and one grey for silver. Maltese is tightly twisted for strength. It is sold on small reels and no longer in skeins.

Filoselle, Stranded Cotton or Perivale Silk. These threads are useful for tacking, hemming, applying ground to backing, transferring design by tacking. They may be used for colour interest in couching though they are not as strong as Maltese silk.

Threads for hand and machine embroidery Silk, Filo floss, and filoselle.

Cotton, Perlé, Sylko thread, Perlita, Stranded Cottons, Soft cotton embroidery thread, Chenille thread as sold for knitting or crochet.

Wools: crewel, tapestry, rug wool of various thicknesses, fresca, mohair as sold for knitting.

Linen threads.

Weaving threads may be used.

Linen or cotton floss may be used for padding small curved areas.

Strong thread for framing-up, for example fine crochet cotton, or linen thread.

Beeswax The sewing thread is drawn over a piece of beeswax which coats the thread with wax to withstand the friction against the metal thread. Beeswax darkens any colour but also eliminates twisting and knotting in the thread.

Greaseproof paper The household variety is ideal for transferring designs by the tacking method, large continuous rolls are available and paper bought in this way is useful for working on designs.

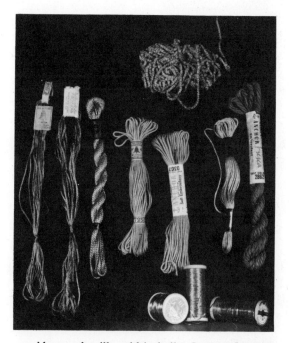

15 Above: chenille sold in balls. Centre: floss silk and filo floss, soft cotton threads for embroidery and padding, stranded cotton and thick wool. Below: machine embroidery metal threads also used for handwork

Acid free tissue paper This is essential for preserving the work in progress and to wrap up gold thread to preserve the quality. Black tissue may be used for this purpose.

Air-tight tin for storing gold threads whilst in use.

Pencil HB and H or HH with a very sharp point.

India rubber

Ruler

Tape measure

Adhesive tape A light self-adhesive paper tape preferably transparent. It is better to avoid an adhesive tape that needs water to make it stick.

Bumph A soft fleecy interlining, or soft old blanket.

Hardboard for stretching finished work.

Drawing pins

A lead weight if available approximately ½ lb.

If making a stretcher:

Wood, screws, metal right angles, screwdriver, gimlet, saw, light hammer, gimp pins, possibly tacks.

16 Thick shiny cotton and rayon thread, crewel wool, tapestry wool, rya rug wool, cotton à broder, stranded cotton, on calico backing

17 Metal right angle bracket, screws for fixing, screw driver, gimlet for marking position of screws and wood $1\frac{1}{2}$ in. × 1 in., shown on a board covered in bumph

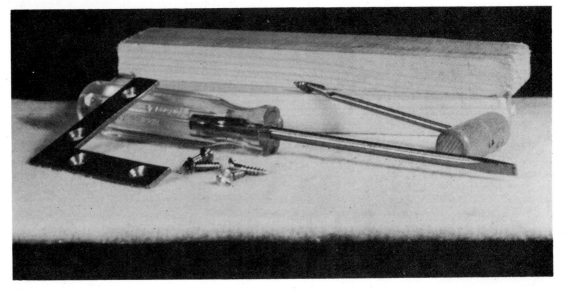

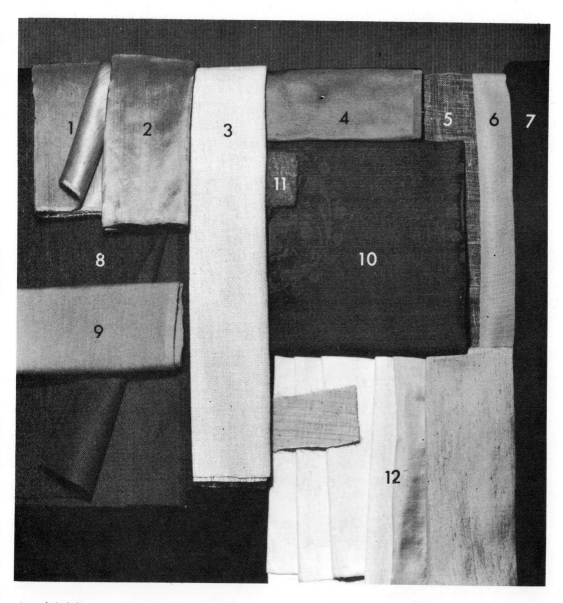

18 1 A bright rayon. Note rough selvedge
2 Sheen of silk
3 White furnishing linen
4 Wool and silk satin mixture with soft rich smooth texture. Note good selvedge of higher quality textiles
5 Thin linen scrim for counting
6 Ribbed repp
7 Heavy matt furnishing
8 Heavy furnishing reversing to twill
9 Medium dull rayon
10 Use of a section of a bold pattern on a mainly plain ground
11 Small area of mohair for possible experiments, texture and contrast
12 Seven different weights of thai silk

Except for firm strong furnishing textiles, most ground materials for metal thread embroidery, and goldwork in particular, need a backing because of the heavy nature of the embroidery which is often worked over a padded foundation and would inevitably pucker the work without a backing.

The weave of loosely woven or light slippery textiles is kept in position by mounting on a backing.

The backing is usually linen of medium weight, that is heavier than handkerchief linen, but is not heavier than the ground except for a hanging such as an altar frontal when dowlas linen is more suitable. A heavy calico or holland are alternatives and these should be shrunk before use. However, so many textiles are now treated before sale that shrinking is not always essential. These backings are also suitable for interlinings.

When experiments with organza or similar material are made a supporting material related to the colour scheme should be used in between the organza and the backing.

'A white or light coloured ground is better mounted on a white linen, as natural colour may show through the ground.

Bumph gives support to the work after completion when being stretched over a board, which avoids a mean look in finishing.

GROUND MATERIALS

Almost any background may be chosen from the bewildering selection of dress, furnishing and embroidery textiles, to serve either as foil to or inspire the design. Lightweight organza and rough furnishing materials cannot be ruled out if the design, technique, scale of work and preliminaries are adapted.

Silks reflect the luminous quality of gold and a matt surface is a strong contrast to the gleaming embroidery.

Plain rich silks, usually containing a mixture of man-made fibre to reduce cost, sell at approximately £2 per yard and have come to be recognised as ideal yet tend to become stereotyped. The silk may be shot with colour, have a small woven self pattern or a definite texture which may influence and perhaps become a feature of the design, such as an experiment with burden stitch on a ribbed

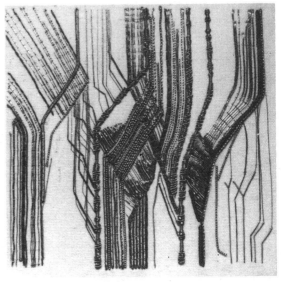

19 A linear pattern worked on cream matt welsh flannel in couched metal threads with string padding covered in close satin stitch as well as purls
Angela Jones

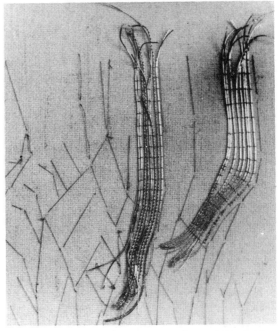

20 Detail, shows a beginning. When working a free design one area is clearly seen in the mind where a start may be made, and the next area worked to complement this. The work builds up in this way
Angela Jones

surface, a counted arrangement of purls on a twill, or open even weave; embroidery linen and scrim may be used for *couché rentré*, or darning.

Thai silks are expensive but are a good choice because they keep their qualities of rich vivid colour, the beauty of softly shining folds and the quiet interest of irregular slubs, replacing ill-designed damasks and brocades.

Inexpensive, under £1 per yard, dress textiles, usually of man-made fibre, tend to split when worked into, though they are often tempting in colour.

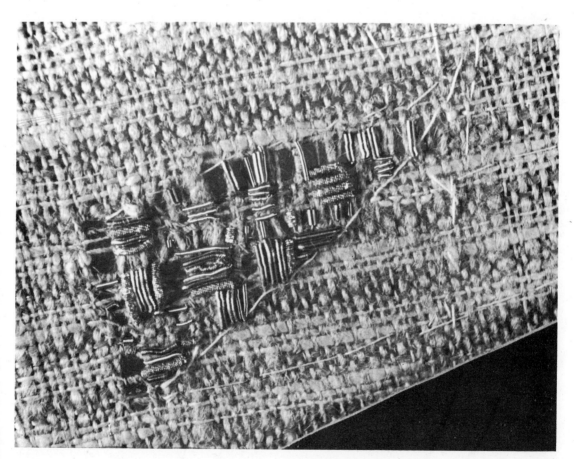

21 Drawn fabric or pulled stitches with purls
Sylvia Haley

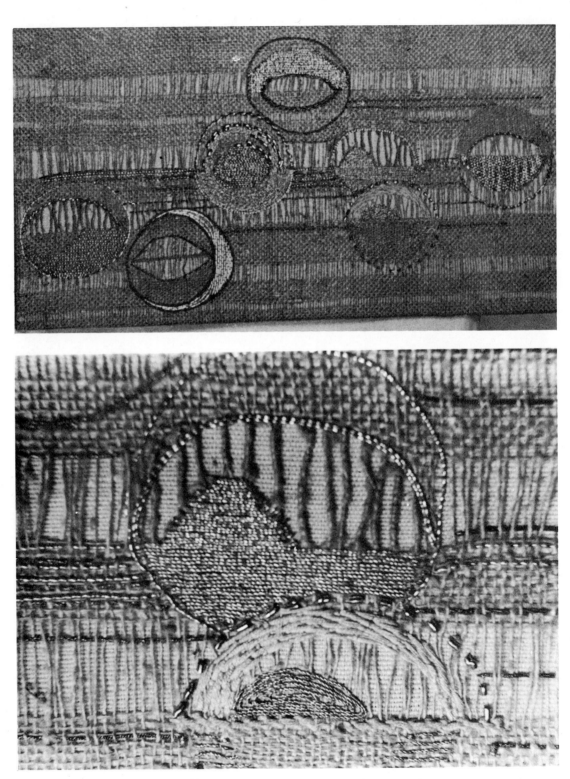

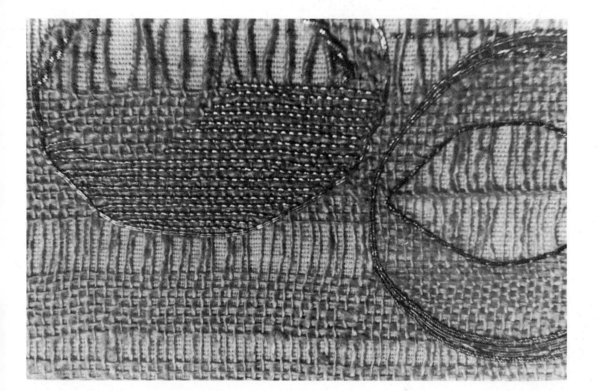

22–4 Embroidery worked on grey green linen with threads in silver and gold. Linen threads are drawn from the background and whipped

Cynthia Prentice

Furnishing textiles may be of a man-made fibre, and inexpensive, but are more suitable because they are stronger. Bold woven patterns overpower the embroidery though a possible use as a ground may be a section of the pattern on a mainly plain ground.

Textiles woven with metal threads may be chosen for lavish results but care should obviously be taken not to let these swamp the work, or the embroidery should be deliberately designed as a secondary feature. Cloth of gold and lamé materials used as appliqué are a possibility to cover large areas of a design in a rich way.

The ingenuity and interest of different workers respond to different stimuli, and this tendency should be cultivated. Beautiful lively or original handweaving add character, and also present problems to be solved by the individual, but in no way should this inhibit the worker and be discarded.

25 Darning patterns in silk and metal threads with
metal thread outline. Compare with similar patterns in *couché rentré* which does not show any
threads of background linen   *Judith Summers*

26 Orange rayon satin with blocks or sections of the design in mauve heavy thai silk makes a vibrant ground for a design based on letters, one curved and rounded, the other straight and angular. The picture shows the strong light contrasts made by a generous use of kid, and though this gives many different aspects to the work, it may also break up the unity of a design   *Anne Spence*

27 Shows use of string padding to state the detail and rows of solidly couched gold to state the shape. The texture of the couching is relieved by rows of twist in different sizes and with silk thread. Note the change of arrangement of couching stitches and that the rows are carefully turned and not taken to the reverse side which avoids weakening this particular material. The mauve thai silk in blind appliqué can be seen at the edge

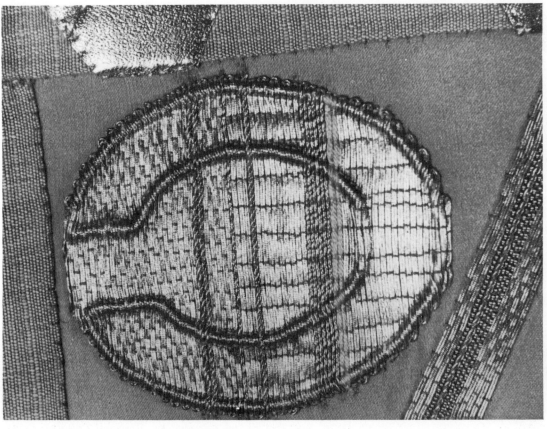

30 Plain parts of orange ground are marked in a controlled linear pattern of back stitch, and further variety in couched gold shows the use of crinkle, twist, and a blocked in border of purl

Opposite

28 Accurate flat gold couching contrasts with the string padded basket pattern in twist. The pattern of blocks, in purl, kid, and couched passing, makes a personal interpretation

29 Further detail showing kid covered with passing and the two backgrounds

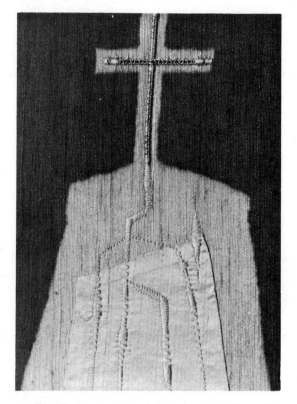

31 Detail, screen printed design with yellow silk blind appliqué and synthetic metal thread held in place by zigzag stitching on a domestic swing needle sewing machine

COLOUR

Textile printing, painting and batik offer other media to be explored for experiments in technique, design and colour.

Gold and metal threads have been used successfully with many brilliant and vivid colours together, similar to stained glass, jewels and enamelling, or with a soft pearly iridescence.

At one time the colours used in ecclesiastical work were limited to a very narrow range, largely through rules laid down by somewhat complicated liturgical ideas. This is virtually obsolete, and a wonderfully symbolic use of colour is made for different festivals and commemorations of the Church.

Heraldic influences recur in embroidery, and here hard, clear-cut lines, colour and shapes are sought after.

Blue and red with no harmonising tone of yellow may make the work appear hard and separate from the ground. This can be overcome by the addition of silk or other embroidery threads in an intermediary colour chosen from the now familiar colour circle, or from a trust in personal colour sense. Chinese work uses multicolours with gold often restricted to outline.

Opposite

32 *Mother and Child* Free batik design in muted tones of green and russet with white. Machine embroidery, hand worked purls and silk stitches (see also 121) *Sister Curie*

33 Design in laid threads and appliqué on silk noiles, and applied repp in khaki colour, threads drawn from the edge are sewn and couched in place. Both sides of kid leather are used with purls and french knots *Diane Bates*

34 Burse. Background of white linen drawn with pulled stitches and lines of gold thread support the cross of padded silver and gold kid, sewn with silver and gold threads, purls and white thread french knots and couching *Freda Tillett*

Opposite

35 Panel suggested by antique fragments, worked in gold threads on slubbed old gold colour silk applied to a backing. Heavy white linen applied over this, frayed out and sewn into background, the lower fringes are mounted on turquoise blue silk. Soft bulky mohair wool in white and turquoise, dull opaque white and turquoise beads add to the texture. The wide inner frame is in old gold gilt and carries the glass, a narrow light colour gilt edging keeps it in place *Barbara Dawson*

36 Detail of 35

37 Detail of 35

This applies, though in a different way, to other colour grounds, when other metal threads are used, such as aluminium or silver which relate well with blue.

Black seems to be associated with gypsy costume and could be worked in dazzling colour and bold braids showing pattern by allowing the background to appear in different quantities. On the other hand parliamentary and university robes are often black only with gold braiding on the sleeves.

White seems associated with the high civilisations, including Egypt, Greece and Peru where heavy gold work embellished fine white linen vestments. Mexican work shows added use of turquoise.

Self colour grounds of cloth of gold or gold coloured silk or other fibre make a rich impact. Dark browns, white, and mixtures containing a rich gold colour, follow the idea of relating the ground colour to the threads.

No rules can be made for colour or background material. Some harmonious colours can be classed as safely successful but tend to become dull and dowdy clichés, whilst too much original colour may become unpleasantly bizarre with metal threads.

Avoiding horrors of this sort is an opportunity for the expression of the talent and taste of the individual worker.

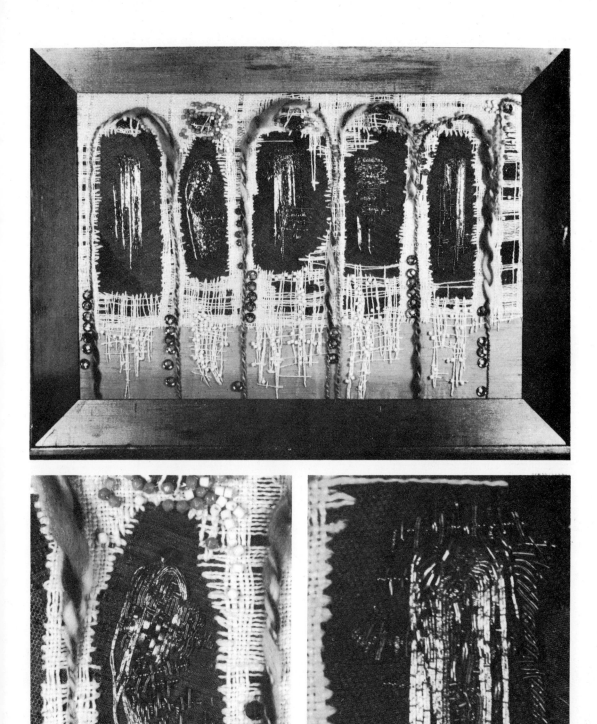

In laidwork threads are laid or passed over the surface of the work, close together. The needle enters the work at one edge, and returns to the top surface at the same edge, next to the first stitch, passes over the work to the opposite side. In this way there is very little thread wasted on the wrong side, and a smooth surface is given to costly threads such as silk which is generally used. The light plays on the different directions of these threads in the same way as on metal threads. Fine stitches usually at right angles couch the laid threads in place. Other decorative methods may be used. Bokhara couching has a similar effect, each laid thread is couched individually as the work proceeds. The threads may be blended and shaded together, and have free or controlled edges. Patterns based on a grid of laid threads seem to have unending variations, and are useful for softening harsh areas.

Appliqué is a French word meaning 'applied work'. There is no English verb *to appliqué*.

Appliqué, like laidwork, covers a large area in a simple, quick economical way. The general rule, and one usually worth observing when applying one material to another, is to match the grains exactly. A template made of the shape to be applied with the grain line marked on it, ensures accuracy when cutting out the applied piece.

To avoid puckers and bumps in the surface, embroidery may be worked on to the larger applied pieces in the form of a seeding, powdering, or a linear pattern to unite the applied fabric to the ground and is usually essential except when the work is stretched taut.

In some instances, when a material of a different fibre is applied to another, it is virtually impossible for any two fibres to react in the same way to atmospheric conditions. Linen, a natural fibre, for example, tends to absorb moisture and become taut, whereas synthetics do not, so that the surface is rarely completely flat. An example, where a slightly uneven surface can become an advantage, is the application of a textile woven with metal threads such as a cloth of gold or lamé. If these metal thread fabrics are absolutely flat, the light is unable to make glinting lights by glancing off the surface and the material then becomes merely a dull brown colour.

Gold or silver kid or other shiny leathers are particularly brilliant and may produce a high white

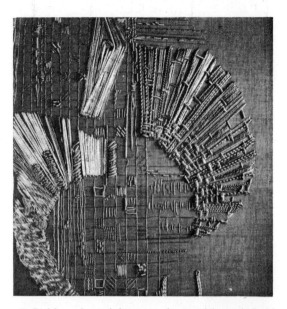

38 Laid work at right sewn down with purl. Laid patterns individually interpreted in a present day pattern *Jo Wheeler*

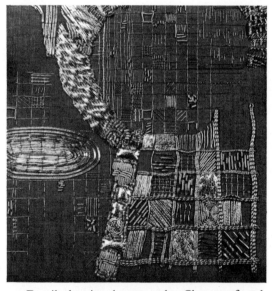

39 Detail showing larger scale. Change of scale reads well in a design as does change of threads and stitch to translate it

shine to dominant for the rest of the textures. The leather is best used in small areas, and worked over with metal or embroidery threads to soften the surface. Laid patterns are ideal for this.

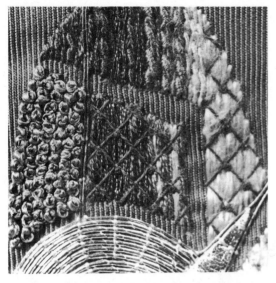

40 More classic form of laid work, but interesting change of colour in laid threads. French knots act as a foil for smooth textures *Margaret Nash*

41 Detail of laid gold as a filling *Mary Rhodes*

42 Laid pattern softens dazzling surface of kid
Marjorie Thomson

35

43 Detail of blind appliqué, backed with stiffening to obviate matching grain on small areas. Note use of lamé material on thai silk and fall of light on folds

Some printed textiles, or those shot with two colours or printed, can add to the design when applied at an angle to the straight grain but these combinations need careful choosing. The rule of matching the grain of the applied piece with that of the ground may be waived when the work is eventually stretched taut. If, however, the work is a flexible hanging such as robes of office, the applied pieces may first be backed with one of the iron-on interlinings, and this is particularly suitable for blind appliqué. The application or fixing of the iron-on interlining to the wrong side of the applied piece requires skill, accuracy and certain amount of flair for handling textiles, and should be avoided by the beginner. The main points to observe are:

1 Make a practice piece first.
2 Whenever possible the shape to be applied should be marked out on a piece of material cut straight with the grain. Lay face down on the ironing board.

3 Lay the iron-on interlining over this.
4 Test the heat of iron. When just hot enough to weld the two fabrics together press (not rub) the iron carefully over the interlining from right to left. Do not disturb the grain of the material underneath otherwise an uneven and irregular surface will occur. Press the iron over again.

Note If the iron is too hot the adhesive will melt and show through to the right side as dark speckling, and if the iron is too cool, the interlining will not adhere and the material will pucker.

5 When the material is cool, tack out the shape.
6 When this method is used for blind appliqué, cut out the shape leaving $\frac{1}{8}$ in. to $\frac{1}{4}$ in. turnings, otherwise omit turnings.
7 Fold under turnings and tack in position. Trim turnings evenly on wrong side.
8 Apply to ground material, lightly tacking in place, matching edge of shape with shape marked on ground material. For blind appliqué, slip hem in place, otherwise oversew.

Frames

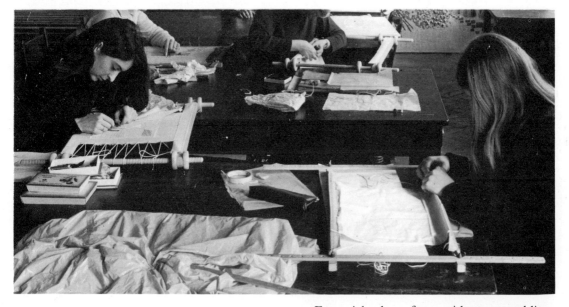

44 Front right shows frame with screws and linen prepared for mounting. On the left, a tapestry frame or frame with threaded sides. Behind, a frame is turned sideways to reach a particular part of the work more easily, notice one hand on top of frame

USE OF FRAMES

Apart from the normal reasons for using an embroidery frame, it is also essential because the method of stretching out the finished work with nails over a damp cloth is impossible as the metal thread would tarnish and possibly blacken with moisture.

A taut frame, which needs regular adjustment when working, serves the following important uses:

1 To prevent the work from puckering when the embroidery is closely and richly worked.
2 To support padded areas and to allow them to rise on the top surface only; otherwise a padded surface appears on the reverse side as in a quilt.
3 To allow metal threads to make accurate turns and retain the sharp outline of a design.
4 To keep the work in good condition and avoid constant folding and handling, if the work is to be carried about.
5 To study the design clearly and accurately as the work progresses.
6 To work from either edge of the design.
7 To allow unworked material to be rolled round lower bar, enabling the worker to reach the centre with ease. As the work progresses the lower part may be unrolled.

In metal thread embroidery, however, it is unwise to roll the finished work on to the top bar or the padding will mark the ground, and other work may be crushed.

Tapestry frames

Many types of square frames may be used (normally made of beech-wood as this warps least), but perhaps the most straightforward to obtain and use is commercially known as a tapestry frame or square frame with threaded sides. It is adaptable, and strong for carrying, but adjustment during work is not so easy as on a frame with pegs.

Note 'Tapestry' in this case is a misnomer used for a certain type of canvas work using such stitches as tent (petit point or gros point) or gobelin, evolved in imitation of tapestry and is a very popular form of embroidery and for which these frames are frequently used. Tapestry is in fact nearer a weaving than an embroidery as the weft is threaded by hand into the warp. Similarly the needle used for canvas embroidery is commercially known as a tapestry needle, having a large long narrow eye to take several strands of wool, and a blunt point so that it does not split the threads of the ground, but slips between the threads of the canvas to make clear sharp stitches.

Square frames with pegs

Another type of square frame, and very popular with professional workers, has sides or arms that may be slotted through the crossbars from top to bottom. The arms are secured in place by pegs or cotter pins, placed in a series of holes in the arms.

This frame is simple, basic and strong, easy to fix and adjust to keep taut during the work.

Square frame with screws

A similar frame, but to be avoided if possible, is one that has screws inserted into the arms. The positions are fixed at regular intervals so that it is difficult for adjustment to make the linen taut.

It is possible to overcome this by framing up extra linen in length and rolling in with a length of soft bulky material as a padding on the crossbar. This is only possible if there is extra material to roll round the bar.

There are other frames with small arms (approximately 10 in. to 12 in. in length), but though somewhat convenient, the frame needs constant tightening during the work. Successful work can result if this is done.

45 Small screw frame. Design linked to brown furnishing fabric by laid gold thread

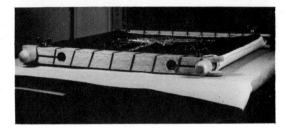

46 Side view of a screw frame

Dressing a square frame for metal thread

1 Mark centre of webbing on crossbar of the frame.
2 Cut a piece of linen exactly to the thread approximately 4 in. larger than the outside measurement of the design. The selvedge should run vertically.
3 Fold under ½ in. at side edges. The selvedge should be snipped, if not cut off.
4 Cut a piece of string the length of the sides and tie a knot at each end.
5 Insert in fold, and keep in place by stitching below string and through the double linen. Start with a small knot and a double stitch.
6 Stitch with running stitches and an occasional back stitch for strength. Finish with a double stitch.
7 Repeat on the opposite side.

47 Back view of screw frame showing extra linen rolled on top bar and soft bulky material rolled in for extra tension

Attach to frame

When using a tapestry frame, with a piece of linen or backing shorter in length than the arms, take four of the wooden rings supplied with the frame and screw one on to each end of the arms, and then insert the arms into the bar, before attaching the linen to the webbing. If the backing is longer than the arms, the arms may be inserted in the same way, but *after* the linen is attached.

1 Fold under ½ in. the remaining 2 sides of the linen and crease in place.
2 Find the centre of the linen by folding in half and matching edges.
3 Match the centre with the centre of the webbing on the bar of the frame.
4 Pin in place using pins upright for exactitude, work from centre to edges, slightly pulling the linen on to webbing. Never ease on to webbing.
5 With strong thread, start with a small knot. Bring needle up through fold. Work a double stitch over the fold and the webbing.
6 Oversew from centre to edge. Finish off by oversewing back on fold for approximately 1 in.
7 Start at centre again in the same way, and work to opposite edge.
8 Work opposite side in the same way. Insert arms.
9 Tighten linen by screwing up arms, or inserting pegs to keep arms secure. Roll extra linen on to the bars.

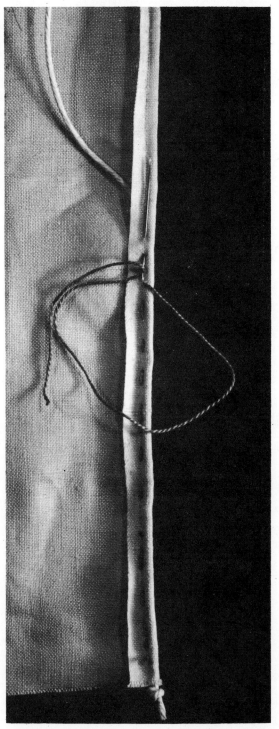

48 String in fold of linen, vertically with selvedge

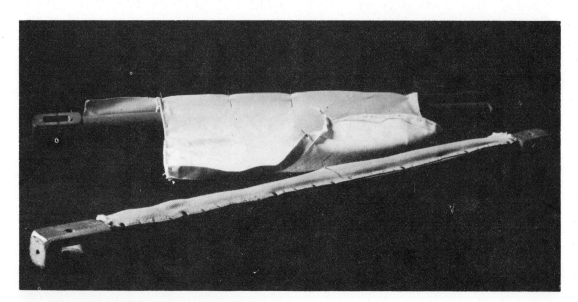

49 With nails towards worker mark centre of webbing on cross bar. Horizontal edges of linen are folded under $\frac{1}{2}$ in. Centre mark matched with webbing and pinned in place. Note string is in both vertical sides and linen gently stretched on to webbing

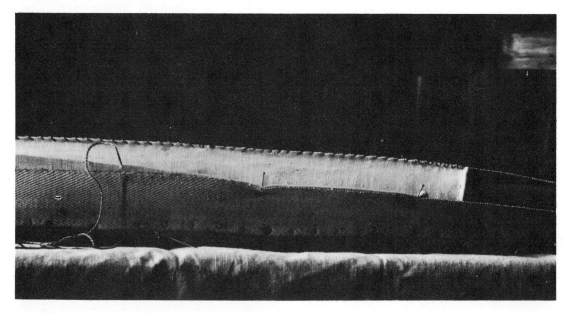

50 Webbing sewn in place, joining thread at front left. At back different directions of stitches from centre and fastening off at edge may be seen. Upright pins in position

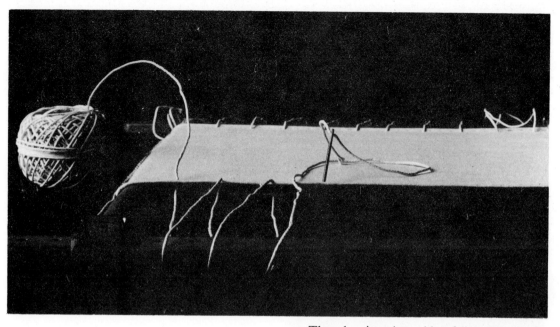

51 Thread strings into side of linen over string reinforcement. Needle away from worker

10 At this stage the linen should be firm but not taut.

11 Thread the packing needle with string, still attached to the ball.

12 Thread into the sides of the linen just over the string reinforcement, pushing the needle down away from the worker. Bring the needle up over the arm of the frame. Leave approximately 24 in. of string and cut from the ball.

13 Work both sides in the same way.

14 Tighten the linen by pegs or screws and by the string until the linen is firm with the frame square and the threads at right angles.

Note This last point can be ensured by a tacking line following the thread of the linen both warp and weft at the centre of the frame. To reduce time and labour the threads may be marked very clearly by tracing a pin steadily along a thread of the linen. Should these lines be askew—check

   1   that the frame is square.

   2   that linen is cut, and the folds are, by the thread.

15 Fasten string with half hitch on the second under lacing.

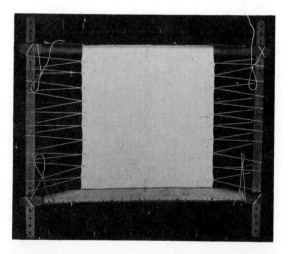

52 Shows a frame with slotted slides and pegs or cotter pins. The lower edge shows full strain of linen on the nails of the webbing, at the top the bar is rolled over one turn so that the bar takes some of the strain. Four pins mark the straight grain. The joining and fastening stitches can be seen, and there is no need for very fine stitches as they are later cut away

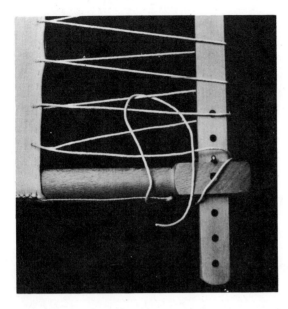

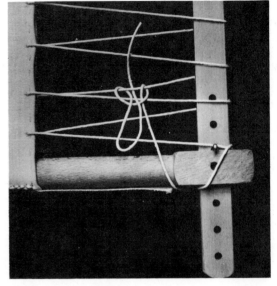

53 To tie knot pass end of string over the second under lacing and bring up towards the arm (sides)

55 Bring end up as a loop

54·Take end over lacing again towards linen

56 Draw up firmly. The knot can only be undone by pulling the end of the string but is otherwise firm

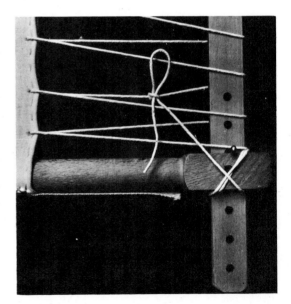

Working on square frames

When working on a square frame, it is necessary that it should rest very firmly and steadily. A pair of trestles are ideal but somewhat costly both in money and space.

Many improvisations can be made, however, such as resting one arm of the frame on a firm table or a window ledge, and the other on the arm of an easy chair, the back of a kitchen chair or between two tables. Any polished surface should be covered with a cloth or some other protection as the frame may scratch the surface.

The worker is then able to sit at the frame comfortably as at a desk, with equipment at one side on a table.

When beginning to work on a frame in this way it is best to work with one hand on the top of the work to pass the needle through to the other side to the other hand underneath. Then the hand underneath passes the needle up through the work to the hand on top for the next stitch.

It is advisable to wear a thimble on the second finger of each hand as each hand is working the needle backwards and forwards, and often through heavy padding.

Working with one hand on top and the other underneath applies even when working on a ring frame, which is made possible by balancing the frame over the edge of the table, weighted with a firm small weight. $\frac{1}{2}$ lb cooking weight, or lead weight used in pattern cutting is suitable.

The manufactured stands for square and ring frames are not always steady enough and too light in weight to take the movements of the heavy stitching. Adjustable trestles are suitable but costly, and take up valuable space in a room.

In a studio or workroom it is considered poor workmanship to turn the frame over and look at, let alone work on, the wrong side, and in these circumstances it is sometimes impossible as more than one worker may sit at a frame, which are often over 6 ft long.

A different treatment is required to start and to finish a thread, when working on a frame than when working in the hand.

To start a sewing thread when working on a taut frame

It is advisable to keep the sewing or couching thread in the needle to approximately 18 in. in length as it needs to be drawn firmly into place for each stitch, and its strength will diminish as it is drawn backwards and forwards through the ground, couched over the metal threads and with the friction against the eye of the needle. A longer thread tends to become weak and wear thin, breaking unexpectedly, where it is not convenient to make a join. When more than one worker is at a frame, a long length is impractical.

It is permissible to start with a small knot—made carefully and quickly with one twist and NOT a number of twists round the finger as used for tacking.

The usual method is to bring the thread through from the under side of the frame passing the needle with the hand under the frame to the hand on top. The small knot indicating the full length of thread, two stitches are made on top of each other (a double stitch) to secure the thread. This should be done on a line or in area of design where it will be covered by the embroidery.

The work is rich and not reversible so that a small knot can hardly mar the right side. The use of the knot avoids bringing the thread right through the material inadvertently.

To finish off a sewing thread

Finish off a sewing thread by taking a double stitch and bringing the thread up to the right side of the frame and snip off close to the embroidery. When working a couched thread the fastening off stitches of the sewing thread occur approximately $\frac{1}{4}$ in. before the end of the line or area, these are then covered by the couched thread when it is taken to the wrong side.

In an area of work the fastening-off stitches can be made where they will be worked over.

When the last fastening off occurs this can be hidden under embroidery already completed.

Mounting ground on to square frame

At this stage the ground material can be mounted on to a slack frame. Never mount a free loose material on to a taut frame as it is impossible to get the two materials, finally, to the same tension.

Cut the ground material by the thread, approximately 2 in. larger than the design. This allows for any expansion of the design and for finishing and bracing. Lay the ground material on the linen.

1 At the centre of lower edge of the linen, approximately $\frac{1}{2}$ in. up from, and clearing, the bar of the frame, match the centre of the ground material.

2 Pin in place at the centre.

3 Thread a crewel needle (approximately size 8) with the equivalent of one strand of stranded cotton, filoselle, or perivale silk in a matching or toning colour of the ground. Start with a small knot and bring the needle up in the linen at the centre and make a double stitch.

4 Insert the needle down into the ground at right angles $\frac{1}{2}$ in. from edge, draw through with the hand underneath to the wrong side of the frame.

5 Bring the needle up again approximately $\frac{1}{4}$ in. along, draw through and insert $\frac{1}{4}$ in. into the ground. This avoids strain on one thread of the fabric, which might otherwise pull away from even stitching.

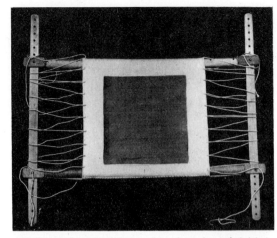

57 Ground material cut by thread and laid in position, matched with thread of linen at lower edge. Stitching started at centre. Note frame is slackened and rolled in at top

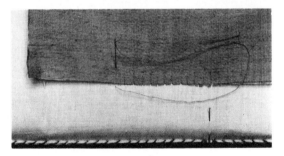

58 Detail of stitching, one stitch $\frac{1}{4}$ in. long alternates with $\frac{1}{2}$ in. stitches to avoid strain in one thread of material. See notes 4 and 5

59 Indicates slackness of frame by weight of scissors, if work is too slack the material works up and down with the needle. Note sewing extends approximately 2 in. up side of ground. See note 9

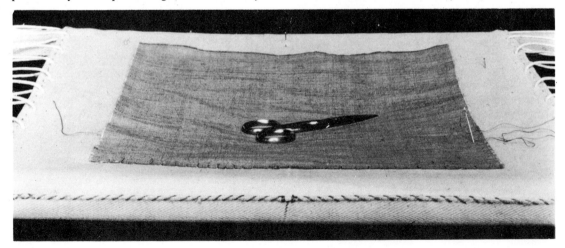

6 Cut off frayed edge an inch at a time.

7 Work from centre to side. It is important to keep the row of stitches straight with the thread of the linen; tack out straight line if necessary.

8 At the side, work up straight with the linen thread for about 2 to 3 in.

9 Repeat at opposite side, and continue to 2 to 3 in. from top edge.

10 Return to the first side and complete to the top edge, and then complete the opposite side.

11 At top edge (the frame may be turned round so that this edge is nearest worker); start sewing at the centre working straight with the thread out to sides. This smooths the material from the centre out.

12 Join off with a double stitch.

13 Now tighten frame both by string and by pegs or screws until it is quite taut and in fact as tight as a drum. Check again that the threads are square. See also figures 62 and 73.

61 Embroidery on strong linen ground. If material does not fit a ring frame an extra length may be added and securely tacked in place

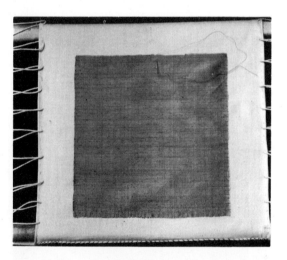

60 At top, start sewing from centre, turn frame towards worker. See note 11

When using a ground material with a pile or similar surface such as velvet the embroidery sinks and crushes the material. The design is blurred and difficult to define, yet interesting for experiments. The difficulties of this type of rich fabric are overcome when the design is framed up and embroidered on a strong linen ground—preferably less coarse, and more closely woven, than dowlas.

If the embroidery does not cover the linen solidly a smooth silk fabric in a colour to suit the work may be applied on to the linen before working the design.

When the embroidery is complete, apply to the velvet.

1 Slacken the frame and cut out the work allowing at least $\frac{1}{4}$ in. margin round the edge for turnings which are folded under and tacked in place.

2 The embroidery is then applied to the velvet, which if possible should be framed up with a backing and with the outline of the design tacked out in position.

3 Lay the embroidery in position on the velvet, matching the most important points of the design and pinning in place. It is preferable to tack all round, if this is not possible catch at these points.

4 Oversew or hem the applied edge in place. If desired the outline may be covered with a cord of gold or silk, or an outline of very free lines of thread couched in place, with the addition of a powdering or purls and french knots, which makes a softer edge and helps the work into the ground.

The foregoing method is useful when experimenting with loosely woven materials or textures as a ground for heavy embroidery.

When couching rows of metal thread on an uneven material a fine smooth linen may be stitched

45

62 Embroidery cut out of frame with turnings as indicated left, hemmed in place and outlined with cord

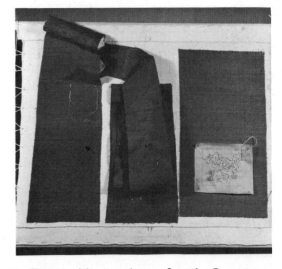

63 Frame with two pieces of work. One an ecclesiastical stole, the other a small panel with traced out design tacked in place

over the surface first. The shape is cut out matching grains and oversewn round the edge of the area concerned.

Another method of making full use of a frame when working several small areas of heavy embroidery, yet obviating repeated framing up, occurs as follows:

1. Frame up a large enough piece of linen to take several pieces of ground material.
2. Apply the ground to the slackened frame in the usual way matching grain. Re-tighten the frame.
3. Complete each piece of embroidery, and then remove from frame as already explained.
4. Lash across the space with strong linen thread to keep the remaining area of linen sufficiently taut for further work.

Adaptations of this method may be used for work which has only one area of embroidery such as a bag, or a stole in ecclesiastical work. The material to be embroidered is cut to shape and placed over the framed up linen. It is preferable to have three outer edges of the ground material stitched to the linen in the normal way, and to use upright tacking on the fourth side. Upright tacking may be used on all four sides but this needs particular care.

In ecclesiastical embroidery, stoles are an obvious use for this method when both ends may be attached to the frame and worked side by side for exact comparison. The remaining length of the stole is left free and carefully folded out of the way of the work except for the seam at the back of the neck which is mounted in the same way for an embroidered motif.

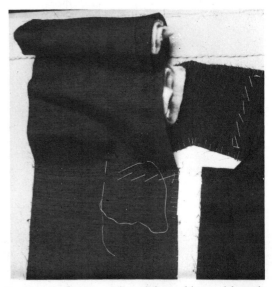

64 Detail of seam and upright tacking, with padding in stole to prevent creasing

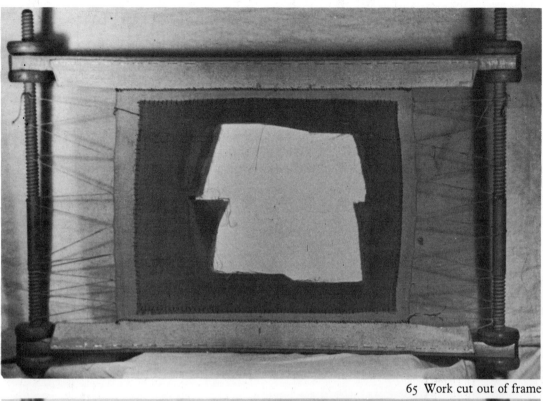

65 Work cut out of frame

66 Remaining ground lashed in position

67 Detail of 66

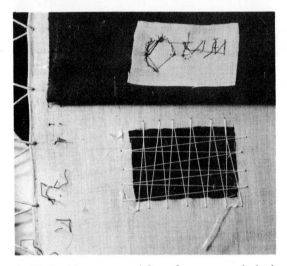

68 Embroidery removed from frame, space lashed across. Note the silk may also be cut but a larger area of silk than linen was required on this occasion

Marking out the design

When allowing the embroidery to develop as it is worked, and there is no set idea, it is preferable that the design should not be marked permanently on the material, such as in the method of pricking, pouncing and painting.

A simpler method seems more satisfactory as the marks are less permanent and are easily adapted to the work as it progresses, giving an accurate interpretation of the design, without marking the ground. Lines marked in tailor's chalk fade quickly.

1 Draw out the main lines of the design on to cartridge or similar paper.

2 On to tissues paper (acid free), or household greaseproof, make an accurate tracing of the design, using a sharp pencil to keep the detail of the shapes.

Note Right angle lines may be drawn over the centre of the design on paper, traced off on the tracing, and thread lines may then be laid over the centre of the ground fabric on the frame. The tracing then laid on the frame matching the right angle lines.

3 Secure with pins at four sides.

4 Use a tacking thread in toning colour of the background or old gold colour, and the equivalent of one strand of stranded cotton, filoselle or perivale. A contrast colour may become worked into the embroidery, and then it is difficult to remove. Tack through the tissue paper on the lines of the design, taking care to mark out corners. Do not use very small stitches as this gives a broken outline. Mark corners carefully.

5 Begin with a small knot and double stitch and end with double stitch.

6 Tear off the tissue paper.

Opposite

69 Design tacked out sufficiently clearly to work with a working drawing

70 Should a stronger line be necessary the line may be painted in. Try outline on spare material

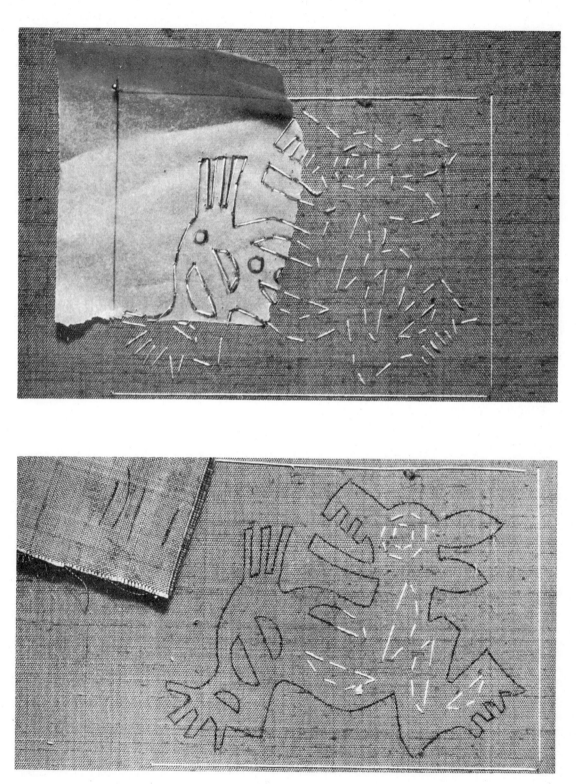

This type of frame is useful if the lack of a square frame prevents a worker from starting on a trial or experiment with metal threads.

It is a quick method when time is at a premium. Very successful results have been achieved in this way if the worker is punctilious in keeping the work taut, but it is very limiting. A backing should be used and the grain matched exactly with the ground material.

1 Place the inner ring flat on a table.
2 Lay the two materials over this.
3 Place the outer ring over the inner ring and material.
4 Press the rings in place.
5 Watching the grain, pull and ease the material in to place with the grain both warp and weft—not bias.
6 If there is a screw on the outer ring, tighten this, and continue to stretch material until taut.
7 Tighten frame as the embroidery is worked.

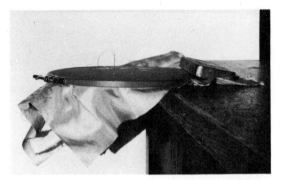

71 Ring frame with material and backing weighted in position, leaving both hands free for working

MACHINE EMBROIDERY FRAMES

To prepare a frame for machine embroidery is similar to above, but the outer ring is placed on the table first, then the material. The inner frame is placed into this so that the material will rest flat and firmly on the table part of the sewing machine.

72 Ring frame with material and backing in position for machine embroidery

As the confidence of the worker progresses and the understanding of materials increases, a simple stretcher may be made by a strongly constructed frame of wood. The size should suit the design and have right-angled corners, which metal brackets help to ensure.

A stretcher from an artists' dealer may be obtained, as used for oil painting, and a backing mounted on to this. Disadvantages are the width ($2\frac{1}{2}$ in.) of the wood which surrounds the work, and also expense, which is greater than one made of narrower wood.

The backing is stretched on to the wood in the following way.

1 Mark centre of each side of stretcher.
2 Cut linen exactly on thread to size of stretcher.
3 Find the centre of each side of linen.
4 Match the centre of bottom edge of the stretcher with centre of bottom edge of linen. Fix in place with drawing pin or tin tack.
5 Pull to outer left edge and fix in place.
6 Pull to other right edge and fix in place.
7 Find half-way positions and fix.
8 Fix at equal positions.
9 Continue until tacks are approximately $\frac{1}{2}$ in. to 1 in. apart.
10 Work opposite edge, i.e. top.
11 Then one side and then the other.

The methods of work are identical to that of an adjustable frame.

Drawing pins allow easy adjustment from slack to taut but tacks need the lifter of a hammer or other tool.

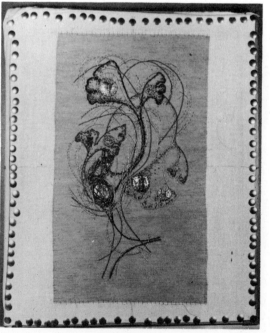

73 and 74 Individually made stretchers in use

51

First work any areas to be machine embroidered and check that:

A The backing is fixed to the ground with upright tacking.

B The design is tacked out on fabric.

C When machine embroidery is completed remove all tacking and cut away surplus backing.

Continue from 1 and adjust design if necessary at 4.

Hand embroidery only

1 Frame up linen backing.
2 Mount ground material.
3 Check that both the grain of backing and ground match, and that they are evenly taut in the frame.
4 Trace tack out design on a taut frame.
5 If areas are to be applied, slacken frame (it is impossible to apply a slack material to equal the tension of a taut frame).
6 Re-tighten frame when appliqué is complete.
7 Pad all areas on a taut frame.

Working on a taut frame

1 Keep pencil to hand in string at the side of the frame to mark in guide lines.
2 Always bring the needle onto the top surface.
3 Keep needle in spare linen at side and not in ground fabric as this may leave a mark.
4 Do not let ends hang underneath, but bring to the top surface.
5 Pieces of linen or tissue paper may be used to protect work from becoming rubbed or soiled at the edge of the frame.

75 Edge of pieces of linen or tissue paper used to protect the work

Padding

One of the chief characteristics of gold is the play of light on the threads, and to increase this areas of work may be padded to raise the surface for adding sheen to the work.

As already explained, padding is worked on a taut frame as if the frame is slack it will sink into the backing like quilting and become flabby.

FELT

1 Areas to be padded are marked out on felt, either by tracing out or by drawing round a template. The thickness of the padding may be varied, and when more than one layer is used the second and third layers are cut consecutively smaller.
2 Place the smallest shape in position first—usually central, but the design may call for other placing, and keep in place with stitches at chief points.
3 Continue with next in size and catch in place.
4 The top layer is complete to give a smooth surface, and after catching in correct position, sew closely round edge. If the padding is not secured at the important points it may shift from the correct placing. Yellow felt is most inconspicuous should any inadvertently show through when working in gold, otherwise match the felt to working threads.

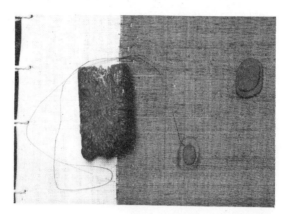

77 Felt cut out ready for fixing first and smallest layer of felt in place with stitches at chief positions. Note beeswax for waxing thread

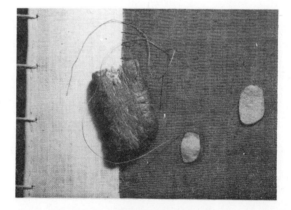

78 Second layer in place

76 Pencil in string. Template for cutting felt and marking position

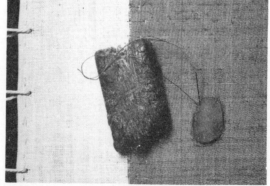

79 Third layer in place and being closely sewn down

53

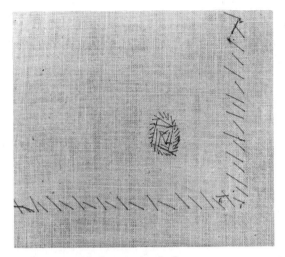

80 Reverse side is completely flat

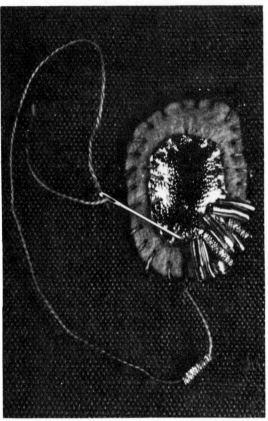

82 Purls sewn round the edge

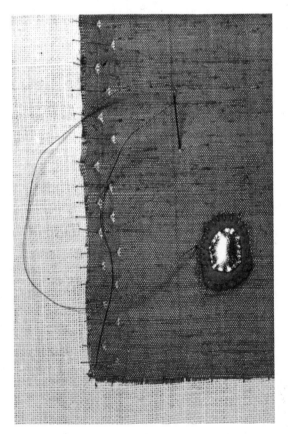

81 Sewing complete and kid added

STRING

String may be used in rows for a filling such as basket work or as a single line covered with purls. Many variations can be worked on this basis.

A smooth strong string is required similar to macramé string, preferably yellow in colour for inconspicuousness. The string is secured about an inch from one end with two stitches from either side into the centre of the string, bringing the needle up in the ground and down into the string, one stitch either side, and then repeat. Continue securing string preferably with stitches forming a back stitch; coming up in the ground and down into the centre of the string alternately from either side.

Tighten the frame if the ground shows signs of puckering.

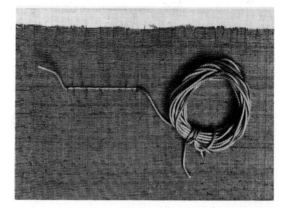

83 Sew string from a length, secure 1 in. from end

84 String pulled gently into place

55

T018123

85 Two stitches from each side to start and finish and alternate stitches from either side

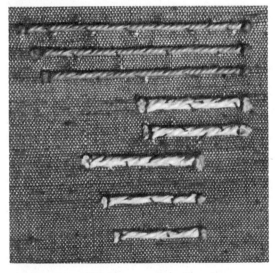

86 Shows method of sewing as a back stitch working from left to right the stitch works from right to left

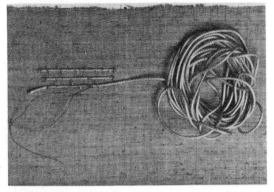

87 A pattern of string complete. See also 113

At the end of the row and before the string is cut off secure the end of the string with double sewing stitches as at the start. The ends of the string are then cut off closely to the stitches, lifting up the end string with one hand to enable the scissors to make a close cut.

56

LINEN FLOSS

Linen floss thread padding can also be used and is suitable for small curved areas such as lettering. Linen floss padding is firmer than cotton, and may be used either as a split-stitch with small stitches into the ground and large stitches on the surface or several threads together couched down. Soft cotton embroidery threads may be used as a substitute.

CARD

Card is another form of padding and serves a different purpose in that it gives a raised yet flat surface with a hard outline. The card is cut to shape and sewn in the position marked on the design. Use approximately four stitches, come up in the ground and down over the edge of the card.

Card is often used for lettering, the metal thread is couched over from side to side, and stitched at each side. The work is often finished with an outline.

Card is also used as a padding to make a pattern in a solid area of metal thread couching. The shapes of the pattern need to be fairly small as the metal thread is passed over the card from one side to the other. Double couching stitches are worked on either side to make an indentation and emphasise the padding.

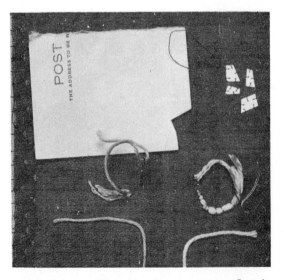

88 Card for padding, also linen or cotton floss in different sizes for padding, either in split stitch for small size, or couched for thick size

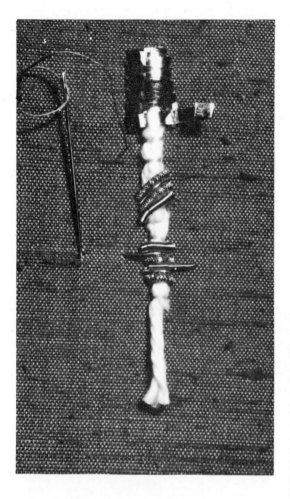

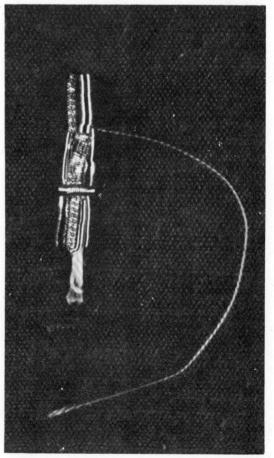

89 Plate at top sewn over padded line. Two methods of using purls

90 Purls on a single line of string padding. See also figures 164, 167, 171, 182 and 193

91 Metal and silk threads over card. Top: a laid pattern sewn in place with crosses of purl. Right: pattern of purls related to the scrim. Below: note corner of couched threads

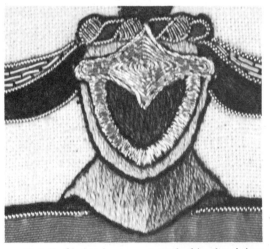

92 Detail of helm, lower part worked in aluminium thread passed backwards and forwards over card, top part padded in felt

Couched Metal Threads

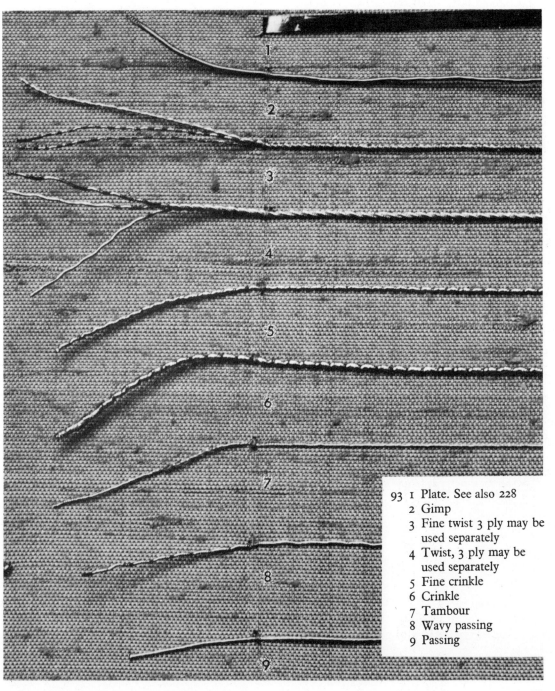

93
1 Plate. See also 228
2 Gimp
3 Fine twist 3 ply may be used separately
4 Twist, 3 ply may be used separately
5 Fine crinkle
6 Crinkle
7 Tambour
8 Wavy passing
9 Passing

These threads are supplied in a variety of sizes, on reels or in skeins of gold, silver, aluminium, synthetic copper and other colours. They are laid on the surface of the work and are couched, i.e. kept in place by small stitches at right angles, in a separate sewing thread.

Passing This passes over the surface of the ground, and thereby derives its name. It is a smooth, and strong, pliable thread, and good for turning corners and angles.

Wavy passing Similar to the above slightly more wavy and less smooth, often finer than passing.

Tambour Very fine thread suitable for sewing through a ground.

Crinkle A textured thread that does not define a corner too well but adds great interest to a couched surface, often sewn singly and used as a cord.

Plate Flat and metallic, bright and shining.

Gimp A decorative thread usually couched but can be sewn into.

Twist Twist is between a fine cord and a twisted thread in two or more plys. Sewn down by slipping a stitch in between the twists from edge into the centre. Preferably as a backstitch and not a running stitch.

Cord Similar to the above but in many thicknesses and can be used very large and sewn similarly to twist.

Imitation jap Tends to appear 'cottony' in comparison, but has many uses.

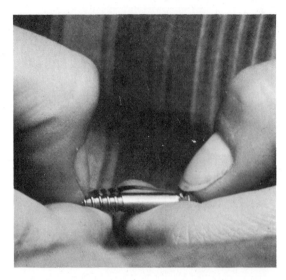

94 Crimping plate on a screw

Soutache A smooth flat plaited appearance, sewn inconspicuously by slipping stitches into the centre from either side, alternately. It may also be sewn decoratively with conspicuous stitches and with the use of purls.

Braids Braids are often available only as a haberdashery or dress trimming and should be used with care as the quality may not be good. This group should not be disregarded as unique textures may be obtained and even though tarnishing may occur, a very subtle colour change is produced.

95 Aluminium threads cut for working

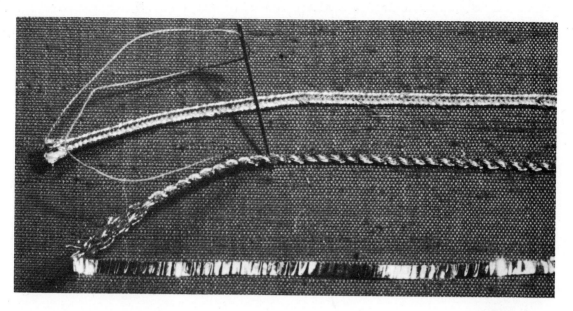

96 Cord
Soutache
Crimped plate

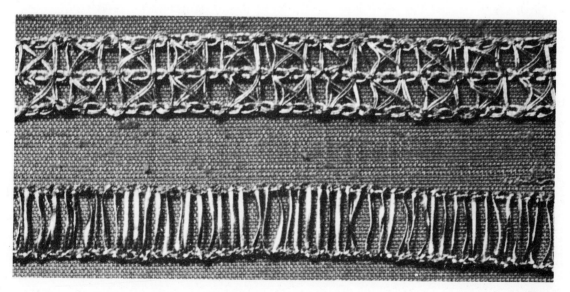

97 Braid

Japanese Gold

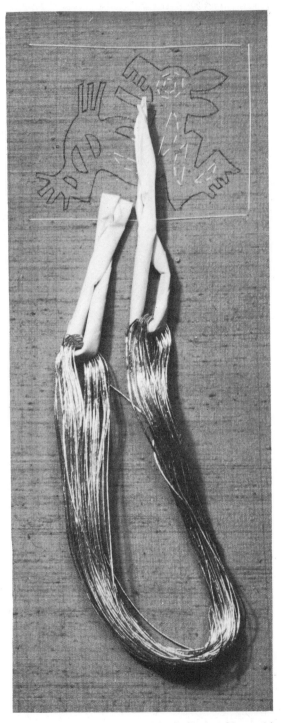

Japanese gold is particularly useful for establishing the main lines of design as it will never tarnish so always gives emphasis to the design. Its rich brilliance is retained when used in conjunction with any of the other gold threads. One thread should predominate otherwise a disorganised texture may result. Jap gold is available in various sizes, but only as couched gold and not as purl. It is unsurpassed in displaying a gorgeous play of light on the different angles and directions of the couched gold. When worked in a design with other threads it is invaluable for stating important areas, as it never tarnishes.

It is made from thin sheets of pure gold beaten out on to tissue like paper, the sheets are then cut into very narrow strips which are coiled round a core of silk floss thread. The silk thread is sometimes a vivid orange, red or yellow and this gives slight changes of colour to the gold thread; further colour may be introduced by the sewing down or couching thread, but the coils of gold should however be kept so close that the silk core never shows. This may require the gold thread to be twisted before and after each stitch, and the sewing thread to be pulled more firmly in place than when couching an ordinary embroidery thread. A 'nipped' appearance should be avoided.

98 Skein of jap gold

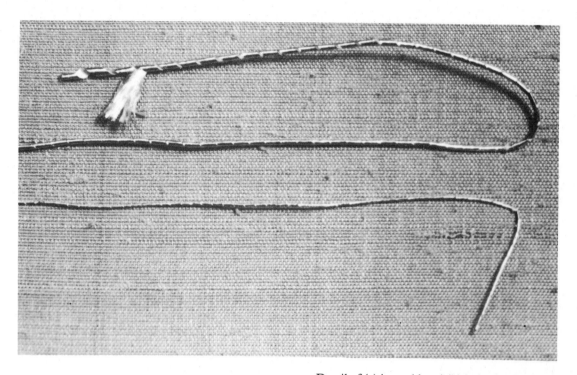

99 Detail of (a) jap gold and (b) imitation jap gold, showing how the lurex turns in a different direction

Note

Japanese gold thread is now virtually unobtainable. A substitute is available and the methods shown here apply equally to this thread. The colour is a rich burnished gold, slightly darker than the imitation jap made of lurex

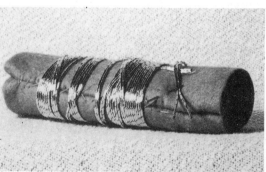

100 Pad for winding jap gold when in use. Note winding in double threads

To Couch Metal Threads

Very few metal threads are sewn through the ground material like an ordinary sewing thread, as the metal thread would weaken the fabric as it is drawn back and forth. This method is a specialised and traditional technical achievement of Turkey and India. There are, however, occasions when the thread is used in this way, such as widely spaced threads, laid fillings, experiments with traditional methods and soft free outlines. See figure 38.

The ends of couched threads both at the start and finish are left free, and are taken to the wrong side of the work when it is completed, using a chenille needle. The Chinese perfected a virtually invisible method of finishing ends, which became their traditional and technical achievement but it is not entirely relevant today.

The metal threads are usually couched down on the surface of the ground material with maltese silk sewing thread. In this way the ground is not weakened by close working and the maximum amount of metal thread is displayed without waste.

When couching metal threads it is usual to couch down two threads at a time for single lines as well as for solid rows (19). This ensures that the rows lie close together and are not separated by the thickness of the sewing down thread, which would show the background in between.

When separate lines are required, a single thread of gold is often too fine and though occasionally used, the double thread answers the purpose more successfully.

Passing is a generally used thread as it is similar to so many other metal threads available, including the synthetic type. When the metal thread is used from a reel, it is practical to measure off approximately 3 yards at a time.

See that the frame is taut and the grain of the ground material straight and at right angles.

1 Using a no. 8 crewel needle join on the previously waxed sewing thread with a small knot and a double stitch.

2 Leave the needle drawn through to the top surface of the frame, take the two ends of the passing and hold in position on the work, with the sewing thread at the side.

3 Leaving approximately 1 in. of metal thread free, take a stitch over the metal thread, and at right angles to it.

4 The metal thread should be held firmly and pulled very slightly tight as the row is worked, and the tying down stitches should also be drawn firmly into place over the thread, so that it does not shift and is not flabby on the taut frame.

5 Continue with stitches approximately $\frac{1}{4}$ in. apart, pulling the metal thread slightly as the row continues.

6 At the end of the row, join off the sewing thread $\frac{1}{4}$ in. from the end, and cut the metal thread approximately 1 in. from the end of the work and leave free.

The ends of couched threads should be left on the top of the work until the embroidery is completed; if they are taken to the underside or wrong side of the work they become entangled with further work and make for confusion. The ends may be tacked to one side on the top of the frame if they are in the way of further work. However, it may be necessary to take the ends to the wrong side before the embroidery is completed in order to assess the work for the next step.

When the ends of metal thread are taken down to the wrong side during the work, it is a waste of time to sew them in place at the back; the ends may be caught back on the wrong side over the work already complete either by tacking stitches or self adhesive tape. This makes a clear working space under the frame and clear view on top and prevents the ends making an uneven surface.

The ends of metal threads are held in place by the firm weave of the backing.

To take ends of metal thread to wrong side

1 Using a no. 18 chenille needle, insert up to the eye of the needle in position where the metal thread is to finish.

2 Hold the needle firmly with the hand under the frame.

3 With the hand on top of the frame put the ends of the metal thread through the eye of the needle. It may be necessary to take one thread at a time.

4 Leaving a loop or length of thread between the eye of the needle and the last stitch, give the needle a sharp pull to the wrong side.

101 Allow a loop to form in the thread between the eye of the needle and the end of the work as indicated, this allows the thread to be pulled down more easily

102 In thick threads it may be necessary to separate the threads—note loop forming

65

Couching

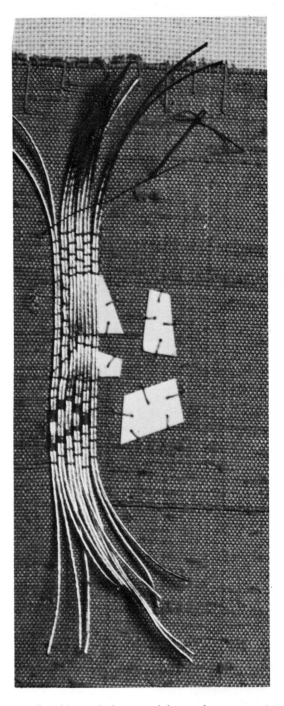

ARRANGEMENT OF COUCHING STITCHES

1 The couching stitches should always be at right angles to the couched thread, and when the couched line is curved the couching stitches are placed at a slant to keep a right angle.

2 In successive rows, the stitches may be placed alternately with the first row. This method is known as bricking, and is generally considered the most inconspicuous method of securing metal thread.

3 Patterns may be made with the sewing down or couching stitches, the simplest being straight rows with the stitches placed directly underneath each other. A simple diagonal is also fairly straightforward.

When more intricate patterns are required the lines of the pattern are marked out in pencil on the area to be covered, and a coloured sewing thread may be introduced.

A development from this basis is known as *d'or nué*, or Italian shading, as so much traditional and historic illustrative work was done in this method in Italy. Another development is known as Burden Stitch.

As much practice as possible should be obtained, so that the threads will be flat, and the couching stitches giving the design sufficient emphasis.

103 Couching stitches at right angles to metal thread in a bricked arrangement and the start of a pattern stitched in a coloured thread which follows a pencilled line

66

104 Couching stitches placed directly beneath each other, laid stitches and purl added for decoration on the couching, jap gold is used here, note stitches at right angles to thread

TO TURN A CORNER OR ANGLE

See also 171, 176, 188 and 249

Making clear sharp corners is an essential part of interpreting some designs, and this requires special thought. Once the difficulties are considered there are numerous ways of dealing with the problem.

The regularity of the spacing of the couching stitches should be maintained and as the corner is approached and the placing of the stitches should be planned symmetrically, to keep the thread straight and not let it bulge.

If the last couching stitch of the line comes $\frac{1}{4}$ in. from the corner, the outer thread is always worked first to define the shape with double sewing stitches at $45°$ (105) as this enables a sharp bend to be made on the thread. The inner thread is then secured with either a single or a double stitch, and the next couching stitch $\frac{1}{4}$ in. from the corner. The last couching stitch of the line may come at the corner, and to take the metal threads round, they are usually dealt with separately (106). A double couching stitch may be made over the outer thread, at an angle of $45°$. This keeps the thread in place and secures it firmly enabling it to bend sharply; a double stitch may then be made in the ground to hold the sewing thread. This stitch is covered by the inner metal thread, which normally requires only one stitch to balance with the other side.

Successive rows at the corner are worked similarly, to keep the spacing regular.

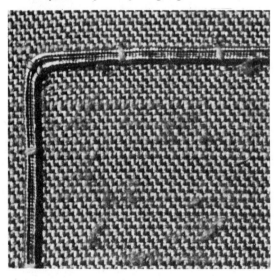

105 Shows corner, note arrangement of stitches

106 Shows alternative arrangement of stitches

SOLID COUCHING IN STRAIGHT ROWS

When working a solid area the first row is worked as explained.

For the succeeding rows bring the needle up in the ground fabric the width of a row from the previous work and insert the needle down against the previous work, and at a slight angle under the row. This helps to keep the rows close together.

At the end of each row it is often just as satisfactory to cut the ends of the couched metal thread, although this entails a number of ends, as to turn the thread on every row.

TO TURN CLOSE ROWS (instead of cutting off the thread on each row)

A method requiring more dexterity, which is acquired as the threads become more familiar, is to turn the inner of the two couched threads back on itself for the second row. Cut the outer thread and lay it alongside on top of the inner thread, leaving the usual 1 in. of thread free before stitching.

Care needs to be taken to get a very neat turn and avoid a bulge in the thread. The awl, or flat side of the blade of scissors or burling irons is helpful in making an angle in the thread.

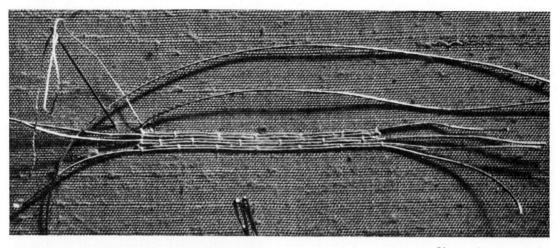

107 Shows slanting needle

108 Shows close rows, note stitches at ends and hidden stitch for strength

There are many methods of turning thread at the end of a row, and variations in the placing of the couching stitches. With a couching stitch in position at the end of the row, an extra stitch may be made over the turn of the inner thread and at right angles to the last couching. To keep end stitches secure, a hidden double stitch may be made, covering this stitch as the row is completed. As the new thread is laid in place the usual bricked couching stitch is made over both threads.

TO WORK A CIRCLE

When working a circle or similar shape, start at the outer edge, as in this way the circle or shape is established correctly. If worked from the centre there is no certainty of the final outer shape.

To keep a smooth outer edge of the circle, the inner thread of the two couched threads is sewn down singly for one stitch. With the second stitch the outer thread is brought in as usual.

As the couching fills the circle, the stitches become very close towards the centre, this is overcome by leaving out alternate stitches on one of the rows.

See also figure 206

A very sharp angle is made by taking the outer thread round the point, working a double stitch at the top, and continuing the thread down the opposite side. If there is not room for the inner thread, it may be cut, and later taken down very close to the top of the angle.

Another thread is then laid in place further down the opposite side of the angle, next to the outer thread, and couched down with it; the end then being taken down later. Succeeding rows are cut at the top of the angle, and started afresh for the opposite side. In this way the threads are dovetailed into the sharp angles.

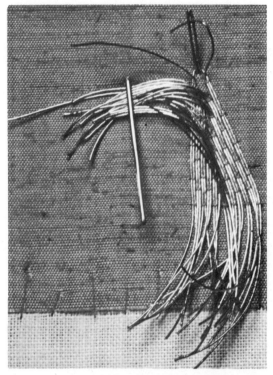

110 One end being taken down

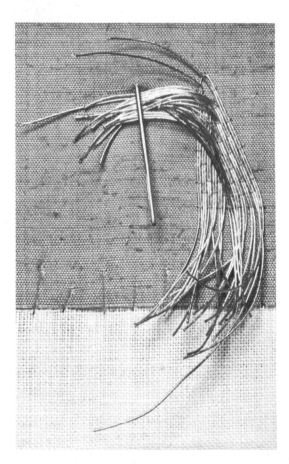

109 Ends of thread fixed to one side to show outer row of couching continuous and inner row cut at top

111 Two ends in place, the third ready for threading. Note at base the use of a single metal thread couched in place to fill space accurately with bricked stitches

112 Point complete, use of bricked stitches

COUCHING OVER A FELT PADDED AREA

Start at the outer edge, bringing the needle up
on the outer edge and inserting it into the edge of
the padding. For the following rows bring the
needle up in the padding away from the first row
and take it down against the old work, as this is less
liable to distort the completed work.

If the rows become somewhat irregular or distorted as the work progresses, this can be corrected
by the addition of extra rows dovetailed into the
shape.

COUCHING OVER STRING

One of the most popular methods on a string
foundation is the basket pattern. This, however,
has many interesting and lively variations, the first
being to vary the thickness of the string, in the
foundation.

1 Some of the rows of string may be quite thick
   contrasted next to a fine string.
2 The spacing may be varied, some rows long
   enough to fill the shape and others shorter.
3 The shape to be filled with basket filling may be
   varied with areas of flat couching at either end
   or with wide spaces in between.
4 Some of the rows of metal thread may be spaced
   leaving the string uncovered. The string is then
   covered later with purls or satin stitch in silk.
   This will mean that some of the ground shows
   through and gives a unifying effect to a design.
5 More than one type of metal thread may be used
   for this work, though one should predominate
   as the pattern will not be sufficiently defined.
   Twist, if used sparingly, adds a contrast to a
   smooth thread, but gives a broken texture
   when worked alone.
6 Silk threads are successful couched in this way.

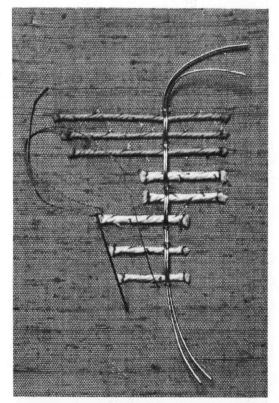

113 Note use of double stitches at start and at
positions between string

1 Sew the rows of string in place as already described, the space between not less than approximately the width of the string.
2 Couch down two metal threads as usual, at the first string take a double stitch. This secures the thread firmly.
3 Pass the metal thread over two strings, and tie the thread down with a double stitch. The stitch needs to nip into the thread, so that a definitely pitted surface results. The frame must be taut for this work.
4 The pattern of couching is repeated to the end of the line. Finish off the sewing thread and cut the metal thread. Leave 1 in. free.
5 Repeat another line.
6 Start the next with a double stitch, but pass the metal thread over one string only, work a double stitch, and then pass the thread over two strings as before. This makes the sewing down stitches between the previous row.

The metal thread tends to spring away from the work if more than three or four small strings are passed over.

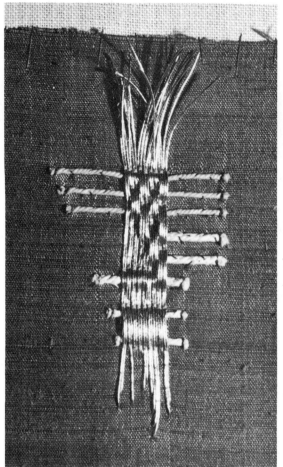

114 An area completed—note closely worked metal threads cover ends of string at centre, where the pattern is flat. Note the top string illustrates how the string will move if not securely sewn and will give discrepancies in the pattern, note also feathered edge at base, and the double stitches either side of the string alternating to keep the pattern

Burden stitch is a valuable textured surface where colour may be introduced in the form of a thicker sewing down thread, and the opportunities for inventing different patterns (228), and different spacings of stitches are innumerable. One piece of work may be entirely worked in this method without being slightly repetitive, and may be worked throughout in purl. See also figure 186.

Lay threads from one side of the shape to the other evenly spaced approximately $\frac{1}{8}$ in. to $\frac{1}{4}$ in. apart according to the scale of work.

1 The threads may be padding threads like a linen floss which are then covered entirely with purl, working in a manner similar to basket filling, but taking a stitch threaded with purl over two rows of string so that the foundation threads are covered.

2 A couched metal thread may be used as the basis, stitched in place first with maltese silk, worked over in purls or with coloured silk and stitches.

When metal threads are laid it is usual to space out the stitches worked over to show the good foundation which may not always need the under couching of Maltese silk.

3 A pearl purl may be used in place of the couched threads, and when worked over with purls gives a very rich texture. See 192 and 193.

In all cases the size of the purl may be varied.

115 Shows an heraldic crest in burden stitch closely worked in shades of red silk over a metal thread foundation to form the mantling. The helm shows a simple example of *or nué* or Italian shading

73

Purls

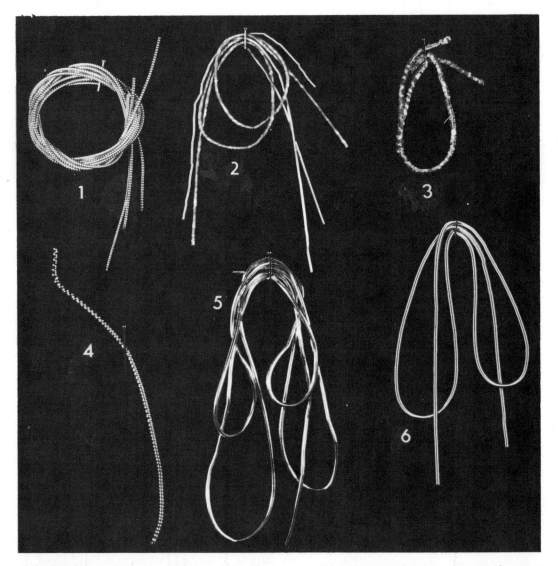

116 1 Pearl purl (wire purl, badge or sometimes bead purl)
2 Small size check, rough and smooth purls
3 Check purl

4 Large size pearl purl stretched out to show stiff springiness
5 Smooth purl
6 Rough purl, note softness compared to smooth purl

There are at least five different types of purls and sometimes these have more than one name. Purls consist of wire drawn out very finely and coiled closely together like a minute spring. They are made in a continuous length which may then be cut to the required size. The purls are pliable and can be cut as long as $\frac{3}{8}$ in. to lie over padded and curved areas. This is an advantage over beads of similar length. Shorter lengths can be used as a close seeding or as a powdering. Care should be taken to avoid cracking or showing a split in the purl as it is worked. Once a rule of this sort is made, an inventive and successful piece of work incurs breaking the rules because the manipulation of the threads is, however, understood first.

Rough purl, in muted soft polished finish.

Smooth purl, a very bright highly polished finish.

Check purl, a mottled sparkling chequered finish.

Bright check purl, similar to the above.

Pearl purl, *wire purl* and *badge purl*.

These names apply to one type of purl where the coil is much heavier and is very slightly drawn out before use so that the sewing thread slips between the coils.

There are few complications in using purl and, having once made a collection of the different types in different sizes, there are endless ways of using them, and playing one with another, such as small smooth purl next to large rough, small check, with large smooth, or all one kind of purl together, but in different sizes.

Purls are cut to the size required by the worker, but not usually longer than $\frac{1}{8}$ in. to $\frac{3}{8}$ in. as this would tend to lift away from the background, though perhaps permissible for a glazed panel in a picture frame.

When cutting purls, which are the equivalent of fine wire, the short tough blades of nail scissors are most satisfactory, as fine embroidery scissors are easily blunted, and possibly bent. Let the length of purl rest on the cutting board, and with the scissors at right angles make a quick neat cut. If the scissors are not at right angles, the edge of the purl will be ragged and a certain amount will be wasted each time. The felt or velvet covering the board helps to hold the cut purl in place, and makes an easy surface for the needle to pick up the cut pieces of purl.

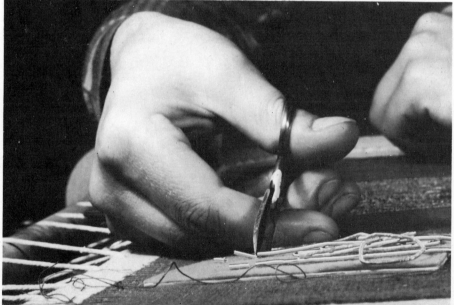

117 Purl cut to size on cutting board. Use of board avoids risk of cutting ground. Make a board by sticking felt, baize or velvet on to card, this helps to prevent purls jumping up when cut

118 Picking up purl from board avoids unnecessary handling

TO WORK PURL

1 Join on a sewing thread of maltese silk in the usual way.
2 Pick up a piece of purl the required size and take the needle down in the position required.
3 Bring the needle up in the position for the next piece and repeat.

Purls may be worked:

1 Flat as a surface filling stitch in geometric patterns similar to counted work, or long and short.
2 Over padded felt with couched gold or appliqué. An entire design may be composed of a variety of padded shapes worked in different patterns of purl.
3 Over padded string as a single line, when the purls may slant to look like a cord or at right angles or actually through the string.
4 As a powdering on the background when they are cut very small.

PEARL PURL

Pearl purl may be given special consideration, because although it is constructed in the same way it is much coarser than the other purls; it is not as pliable, and it is only rarely cut into short lengths for covering a surface. When this is worked with the pieces slightly over-lapping one another in an irregular pattern, it gives a strange surface as if composed of minute sticks.

Pearl purl, usually couched in place, is available as is the other purl in many sizes, but there are three sizes more distinctly made as there is an extra small size known as super, extra or minikin, the other end of the scale being the large size known as bullion.

Pearl purl is ideal for introducing into rows of couched gold as it gives a lovely textured line, for lines and outlines.

Pearl purl may be manipulated into sharp

76

119 Shows pearl purl being held in place for sewing down—note use of two thimbles

corners and make accurate detail to define shapes and give a neat. outline which is sometimes required such as for heraldic charges. The ends of pearl purl are cut flush, and rest on the top of the work, as it does not fray, and so, in this way, none is wasted.

Pearl purl may also be used as a basis for Burden stitch.

TO COUCH PEARL PURL

1 Stretch the coils of pearl purl open sufficiently to enable the sewing down thread to slip in between. This makes the sewing down thread virtually invisible.
2 Arrange the first stitch into the first coil—do not leave any spare.
3 When working a continuous outline, cut the pearl purl so that the end will meet flush with the beginning, arrange a stitch into the last coil.
4 Finish off under the wire.

The wire may be pulled out in parts until it is nearly straight and this gives an interesting line of varied thickness.

Spangles

120 Spangles and jewels attached in different ways

Spangles are sewn on the surface and differ from sequins in that they are flat and have a small split on one side to the centre hole, both are used as a filling or a powdering. Sequins are slightly faceted and glint more dizzily than spangles which flash with light.

Jewels and Beads

Jewels are obtainable in various forms and colours, and may be used to highlight the work. They may easily alter the character of the work, if not used sparingly, as they are usually made of glass or plastic, and often appear crude. There are many inventive ways of securing jewels in the work, the most usual being to work over the sewing down stitches with purl.

Gems

Gems are an expensive accoutrement to embroidery, and would seem to need very special and personal requirements; though no doubt adding a genuine richness, jewels, gems, beads and sequins tend to by-pass the real substance of embroidery.

121 Detail showing cable stitch used to strengthen lines of design. Delicate handwork in the form of purl, spangles, floss silk and french knots relate to the fine lines of batik

STRAIGHT STITCHING AND TEXTURES (124)

When using metal thread with a sewing machine the thread can only be used on the spool (bobbin or shuttle) which is inserted into the lower part of the machine, and not threaded on the top and through the eye of the needle, because the metal thread would not pass through the eye. The top tension is threaded with either machine embroidery thread, or a fine silk thread, and the tension tighter than for normal sewing.

The metal thread must run easily off the spool. If either tension is too tight the thread will snap and break, and the solution to this is to keep the metal thread running smoothly and freely. However, a loose top thread may also solve this problem, and it can produce a very interesting texture, although not technically or mechanically correct.

The length of stitch is usually increased for this type of work when separate or isolated lines are used. An average or short length stitch worked in close rows makes an allover textured filling of the metal thread.

If the tension is made irregular, the sewing thread may show through on the right side and this can add to the attraction of the filling.

This texture is suitable for working in conjunction with hand embroidery, either as an area in a design, or as a foundation upon which to build more encrusted texture and detail with metal threads manipulated by hand.

79

CABLE STITCH (machine couched thread) (32, 121, 122)

122 Shows very simple lay out in machine cable stitch in gold which could be the basis for further work

Cable stitch may have a slightly thicker metal thread than that used for texture, and a larger stitch. As the metal thread is the under thread on the machine, a loose tension is required. The work is controlled from the wrong side of the work, and this means that if a design is to be traced out, it must be done on the wrong side as the right side is face down on the machine.

1 It is advisable to back the material to be embroidered with scrim, mull or organdie.
2 The backing, with the design already marked out, and with the grain exactly matching that of the ground, is fixed in place by upright tacking.
3 Work the tacking rows from top to bottom, and from left to right, until the two layers are smoothly joined as one.
4 The work is then placed in position in the machine, right side down, and the design uppermost, the foot is lowered.
5 Whenever possible, the lower thread is brought up to the top surface, to avoid a congestion of threads, except when thread is too thick, when it should be held to one side underneath. At all times the two ends should be held out of the way, at the start of a line of stitching.
6 Follow the lines of the design with lines of machine stitching.
7 It is essential to keep an even speed, as otherwise the thread is jerked and may break.
8 To turn a corner, lower the needle in position, raise the foot, turn the work, lower the foot and continue.
9 To fasten off, when the material is substantial, the ends may be knotted, but if very lightweight, the sewing thread should be sewn by hand over the metal end, and into the backs of the stitches on the wrong side.

SWING NEEDLE (31)

The swing needle, or zigzag sewing machine may also be used while the foot is in position, by securing the metal or synthetic threads, with a zigzag stitch.

A smooth flat thread similar to a soutache braid is ideal for this, as the edges may be sewn into. If the thread is round or narrow and now stitched into in any way, it tends to shift out of place, and become loose and wavy.

A backing should be used as before and great care taken not to stretch the work on the bias, as the thread is unyielding and will keep the ground fabric distorted.

Another method, using trade machines or domestic sewing machines when the foot should be removed and the feed lowered or covered with a plate, is to execute the embroidery in a ring frame. See also 50.

The machine is threaded as before, keeping a loose tension for the metal thread on the bobbin.

A taut frame, or working area, is an essential part of the successful stitching in this type of embroidery.

1 The design should be traced on to the backing, and this, with the ground material, carefully matching the grain, should be stretched into a ring frame.

2 With the outer ring flat on the table, loosen the screw of the frame, and lay the two layers over this.

3 Press the inner ring down into position, gradually stretching the material taut and tightening the screw at the same time.

4 The two layers must be evenly taut in the frame, and this may involve pulling the backing separately from the ground material. Care must be taken not to distort the grain in the frame by pulling the material on the bias.

5 With the right side face down, insert the needle into position on the design, turning the mechanism of the machine by hand. Bring up the lower thread whenever possible as previously explained.

6 The design or the working areas should be carried out with a very steady speed and an even movement of the frame. The length of the stitch is made by the speed of the moving frame.

7 Finish off as before.

Metal thread machine embroidery may be worked into with hand embroidery using the usual embroidery threads, or another machine method such as whip stitch, using ordinary machine thread.

WHIP STITCH

Whip stitch requires a tight top tension and a loose lower tension and is worked on the right side of the material and in a frame. This produces a neat raised corded line and can be used in many ways.

A second method is to fill a spool with a fairly thick embroidery thread such as perle or soft embroidery. Have a very loose lower tension, even

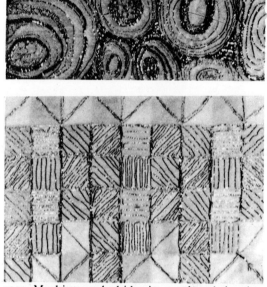

123a Machine-worked idea in one thread showing how the light on the different directions of the thread changes its appearance

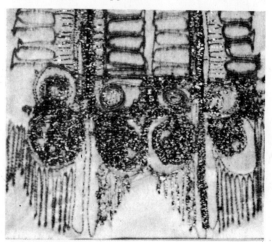

123b An idea for machine embroidery showing whip stitch in ordinary thread with metal thread textures

removing the tension band. The top tension is slightly tighter than normal, and a fine machine cotton is used.

The stitch is worked on the wrong side, and produces a raised thread of uneven thickness on the right side.

The work is prepared as previously described, and with a frame for free working.

81

123c An idea for the machine from a seed head, on ribbed silk

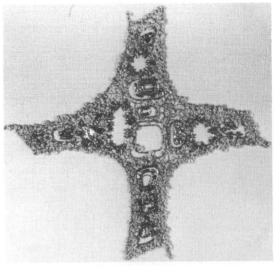

125 Machine perlé and metal thread and purl

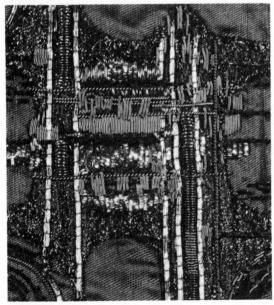

124 Machined metal thread texture amplified with handwork in purls and jap couching

126a Detail shows thick and thin threads in machine embroidery with handworked couched crinkle thread and purls

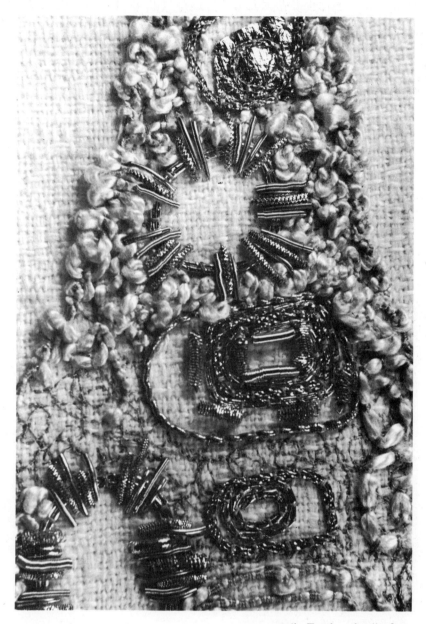

126b Further detail of 125

Finishing

127 Trim ends of work on wrong side

Metal thread embroidery can never be damped and stretched, except possibly a novelty synthetic thread marketed for washable dresses or table linen.

When the embroidery is completed and the work still on the frame it is then permissible to turn to the reverse of the frame.

1 Trim the ends of the metal threads to $\frac{1}{2}$ in. to $\frac{3}{4}$ in., and press back against the area of work. If the ends are left to lie under an unworked area of ground there is a tendency for them to make a lumpy surface.

2 With the work still taut on the frame and with the wrong side uppermost support the frame so that right side work is not in contact with a surface, and press lightly with a fairly hot iron over the back of the work. This helps to settle the stitches in the work, and give a crisp finish to the right side.

3 Leave the work to cool, as if it is taken out of the frame whilst still warm any creases tend to become permanent. The work is then ready for mounting or making up.

4 To cut hardboard for work to be finished by mounting in a picture frame, allow $\frac{1}{2}$ in. extra to the finished size of the design for the work to rest in the margins comfortably.

Otherwise mount the work, preferably close to the edge of the design: the hardboard should be cut approximately $\frac{1}{4}$ in. smaller all round. The bulk of the backings will make up the extra size.

5 (i) Cover the hardboard with a piece of bumph or old soft blanket to give support to the work and to avoid a meanness in the finished appearance.

(ii) Cut the bumph approximately $1\frac{1}{2}$ in. larger than board.

(iii) Lay the pitted side of the hardboard to the bumph, so that there is an even margin of cloth all round.

(iv) Fold over one edge to the smooth side of the board and fix in place with adhesive tape.

128 Arrange ends and trim bulk at corners. Keep in place with adhesive

(v) Turn board pulling bumph firmly over opposite edge, fix in place similarly.

(vi) Arrange the ends and trim away extra bulk at the corners, then cover the ends of the board in the same way, fixing one, and pulling on it for the opposite one.

6 When removing embroidery from a taut frame it is essential to slacken the frame first, working in the following order.

(i) Loosen and remove string.

(ii) Slacken screws or remove pegs.

(iii) Snip and lift out the stitches attaching the work to the bar of the frame. (Do not cut one stitch and drag the remaining length of thread through the work to undo the stitches, as the pulling may distort the material.) Remove the dead stitches.

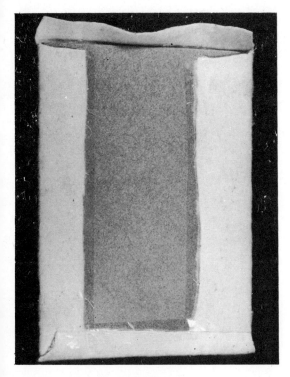

129 Note corners cut away

(iv) Cut away the linen backing, close to the ground material.

7 Lay a soft cloth on the table surface and with the embroidery right side down, mark the centres of the edges on the wrong side with a pin. Lay the covered board over the wrong side of the design, matching these centres with the centre of the embroidery edges.

8 Along one edge of the board, fold over the surplus material of the embroidery and pin in place with an upright pin, through the fold of the material and the bumph foundation.

9 Fix the opposite side and then the third side and finally the fourth.

10 Turn to right side and correct placing of work if necessary.

BRACING THE WORK

Use strong linen thread or crochet thread.

1 Thread a needle (size 5) with thread from the reel or ball (do not cut a length).

2 Insert needle at the centre edge of the work through the backing and the ground, as for herringbone stitch, draw through. Work a stitch on the opposite side. Continue to end, working from left to right, drawing off more thread from the ball as required.

130 Work pinned from wrong side is turned to right side for checking correct position and margins

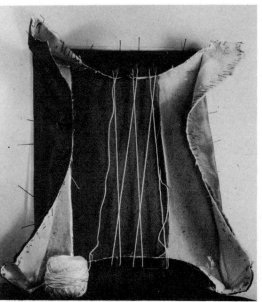

131 Note linen cut away close to edge of ground. Thread bracing work start at centre with thread from ball

3 Fasten off thread with double stitches. Cut the thread from the ball leaving approximately 12 in.

4 Turn work, and work in the same way from centre to the other end, but do not fasten off. Leave 12 in. at corner.

5 Starting at the position where the thread is fastened in the first corner, draw each successive stitch firmly to the centre, and knot tightly with the thread of the second half, leaving as short a length as possible between. Cut off surplus thread. Continue drawing the bracing stitches firmly into place, and fasten off at opposite corner.

6 Work the sides in the same way.

7 Do not cut bulk away from corners but fold neatly into place, and stitch in position.

If the material is cut at the corners the work cannot be remounted should this be necessary for a different purpose. Cutting also weakens the materials.

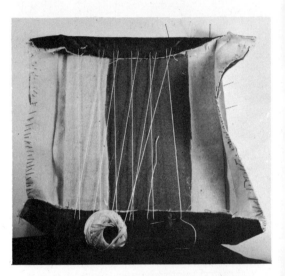

132 Thread fastened at bottom right now at top left as work is turned, and braced to lower left again. Threads joined at centre but ends still separate

133 Draw up stitches from left, knot ends at centre, draw up to right and join off securely

134 Working short sides over long repeat as before. Do not cut or trim corners. The corners may be slip stitched in place

86

When the ends of couched metal threads are taken to the wrong side it is unnecessary to sew or stitch them in place as the close weave of the backing and the ground keeps them in place.

If the ends of the metal thread are particularly springy and do not lie flat on the reverse side, they may be kept in place by adhesive tape.

When floss silk embroidery has been combined with metal threads, it is often wise to keep the work in place on the wrong side by passing a very light layer of adhesive solution over the backs of stitches.

In the past this has been done by securing a sheet of fine tissue paper over the back of the work with paste, not always satisfactory as unless correctly mixed may moulder. Nowadays, with so many excellently made rubber or similar clear transparent glues available, the problem can be solved more satisfactorily.

In addition to the adhesive, a layer of tissue paper may be fixed in place over the back of the work.

BOARDS

The boards on which to stretch the completed embroidery as a wall panel should be particularly strong. A fine hardboard is the best basis.

Hardboard neither bends nor curves in the way that cardboard or strawboard tends to, nor does it split and crack, as lightweight wood might.

LINEN

Heavy linen or tailor's canvas may be used as an interlining for embroideries to be treated as flexible hangings or textiles.

In this a lining is used to cover the reverse side when complete.

This method encroaches onto the subject of making up, and goes beyond the present subject.

PICTURE FRAMES

Picture frames with glass are perhaps one of the best ways to avoid discolouration of thread, as the work is protected from the atmosphere in a nearly airtight case.

The choice of frame is important and can easily mar a work by being too heavy and overpowering or becoming too slight to support the work.

A cardboard surround always seems comparatively too cheap a finish, and the work would be better displayed unframed.

Design

Metal thread embroidery may have any feature or aspect of design, and diverse interpretations prevent a recognised and stereotyped style. Linear pattern or solidly worked designs carefully controlled or freely arranged may be equally successful, with the introduction of colour for sumptuous effects. Metal threads add brilliance to other embroideries such as canvas or drawn fabric provided one of the techniques predominates.

Whilst it is impossible to lay down rules of how to make a design it is interesting to clarify ideas which may be applied to design generally and to embroidery in particular.

A parallel may be drawn between an embroiderer with a talent for expression in threads and textiles, and a draughtsman with a talent for expressing in pencil and paper the forms being studied. A good likeness, and good techniques may result, but they are merely ends in themselves if there is no sensitivity or experiment to exploit the medium, state character or atmosphere, originate an idea or show a sense of design.

An insistence on evidence of good draughtmanship before attempting design would become another rule and therefore questionable, for many good designers have a talent in excess of drawing ability. The designer or painter will enrich his work by studying drawing and developing nuances of tone, line and texture, but there are few who are gifted with an ability to see form and translate it immediately into design.

Describing and explaining designs, though agreement with what is mentioned is not always possible, may be a spur to those who need to work further at design.

The drawings by Rembrandt (135–141) show the value of drawing coupled with design and of the use of tone and line and the endless possibilities of treating a subject in relation to the background. The variety is so clear that it is easy to see how this may be used in embroidery.

135 *The bust of Rembrandt* self portrait on a plain light ground. Dark areas account for a very small part of the picture but forcefully state the form and lines suggest form in the light area. Note a dark eye on light and a light eye on dark

136 *Woman teaching a child to walk* A pattern of lines on a light ground

137 *Study of a woman bathing* A patterned background of great variety with some areas softly shaded and blocked in, others in close lines. The subject is virtually plain with only differentiation in thickness of outline

138 *Virgin and Child seated near window* Wonderful areas of plain light background which could be abstracted as a rectangle along the bottom edge and another in the window. Other areas are patterned in tone as is the subject

139 *Two men's heads* This shows how small intricate work can be rewarding. The large bold confident strokes state the right hand hat whilst meticulous lines give entrancing detail. Note contrast of noses

140 *Study of a Lion* Animal drawing with a feeling of repose yet with evidence of ferocity in the claws

141 *Elephant* The weight of the elephant shown in the heavily shaded legs and the fine line along the head and back make a feeling of unlimited bulk contrasted with the scale and line drawing of the figures

The brass rubbing shows a strength of design in the well drawn figure and the use of a cruciform shape and the different ways in which it has been treated. The change of scale from the narrow border in the arch of the canopy to the bold rectangle at the hem of the alb; the curve of the folds of the chasuble opposite the maniple are repeated in the carved edges of the canopy: the pointed arches of the architectural forms are repeated in the figure by the hands in prayer, the shape itself is sometimes black and sometimes white and counterchanged in a negative-positive way on the background. The chalice is echoed in the curved line of the amice round the neck. Perhaps in passing it may be mentioned that the monumental brass is dated 1361, which is the date of one of the outbreaks of the Black Death with the elimination of so much of the population and with the eventual discontinuance of the famous *Opus Anglicanum*, so that the vestments depicted may be of the highly prized metal thread embroidery.

To permeate design with the present time of the worker, a study should be made of the typical forms of that time. By drawing and observing the buildings, machinery and scientific inventions of our own time a copy of past ideas is avoided. A simple example of present-day influence is to be found in the large lettered instructions and advertisments.

If these are read as pattern, and not as words, many related shapes may be seen. The universal love of perpetuating animal and plant form becomes an occasion to study design within natural form, so that the appeal is retained and a good design is achieved.

In this way the awareness is sharpened and it is realised that design is not an interpretation of an enchanting subject attractively drawn, or an imaginative rendering of movement expressed in an abstract way.

Illustrative work telling a story has been generally replaced by reading abstract shapes in the mind, or with the senses and intellect in a way that gives a wider appreciation and the opportunity for many interpretations. What may be seen as wild confusion may be seen by others as liveliness, and classic stillness may be seen as deliberate restraint. The design may become so highly developed that the foundation or basic ideas are no longer recognisable.

142 Brass rubbing of William de Kestevene from St Mary's Church, North Mymms, Hertfordshire

Foundations are necessary to a design, and when a feeling for threads and embroidery is greater than an ability to draw, a beginning may be made by cutting out a shape in paper, and then devising variations by cutting it in different sizes, elongating it, making it narrower, shorter, broader and finally placing the shapes into a plan or pattern on paper. Further planning may be carried out by placing the shapes in relation to each other, the outer edge and by introducing a complementary or contrasting shape.

143 Shows an individually cut out shape repeated with great invention and arranged in rows, making a simple design with interest. This design or pattern could be treated in many different ways either by working the shapes solidly or as an outline or by working the background leaving the shape plain. The background could be worked in rows horizontally, vertically or round the shapes using couching line stitches, counted patterns of variations of powderings or seedings

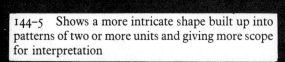

144–5 Shows a more intricate shape built up into patterns of two or more units and giving more scope for interpretation

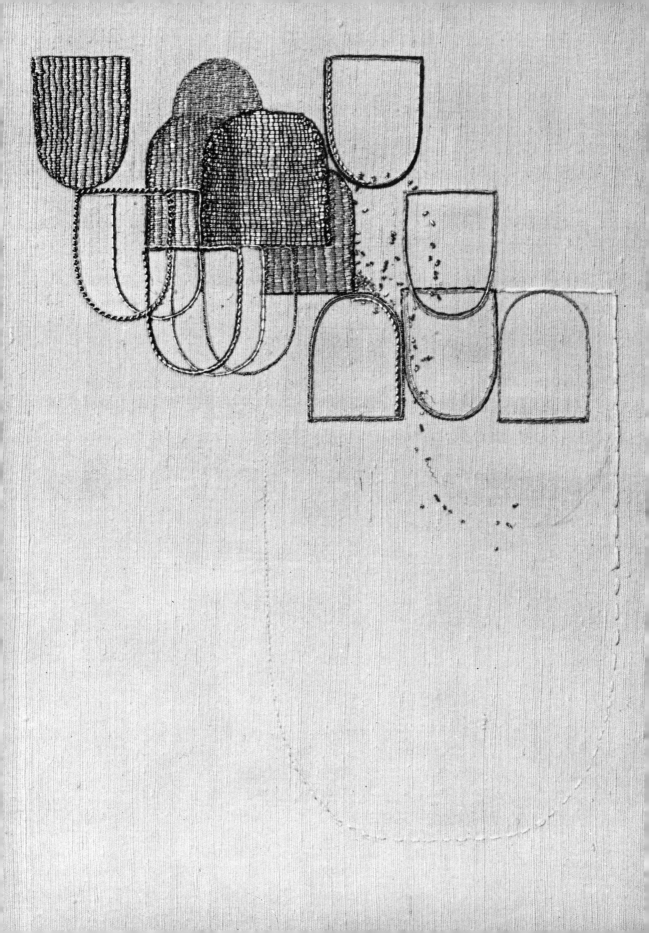

146 A design planned with a simple shape which is overlapped to give variety. The embroidery emphasises the solid shape and also the outline and the interest in the new shapes made by the overlaps.

The solid filling shows the use of *or nué*, or shaded gold, in this example shaded silver. The colour of the couching thread is changed to indicate separate shapes. The metal thread is turned at the edges; this makes an edging or border and eliminates taking down the cut ends of the metal threads.

The linear shapes are worked in different types of metal thread and include pearl purl, twist and passing, with the addition of couching or stem stitch in the coloured silks used for shading of solid areas.

The comparatively large empty space beneath the design complements and sets off the intricacy of the work. The shadow of a shape falling away in run stitch is in silk thread to match the natural silk background

Stephnie Tuckwell

147 Detail

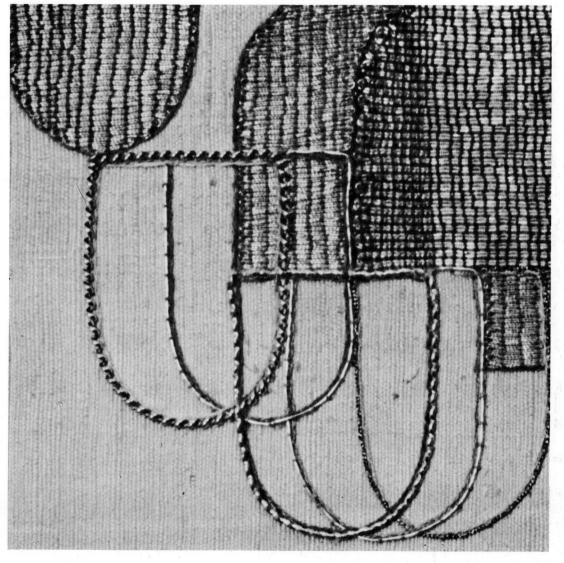

148 A design from scallops, shown as a repeating pattern at the base, and freely arranged at the top.

Worked on a mauve shot silk background with couched threads and smooth, check, and pearl purls in silver, silk and cotton threads in mauves and sand colours are used for satin stitches and french knots.

The purls are used over padding, and pearl purl as an outline, together with silver passing for solid lines at the top with rows of different coloured silks.

Purls are added to the seeding and run stitches in the background *Jackie de Courcy*

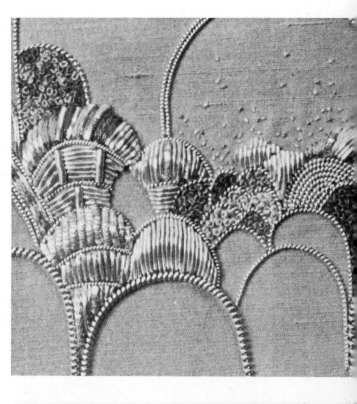

149, 150   Details

151 Working drawing ready for tacking out.
See figures 69 and 70

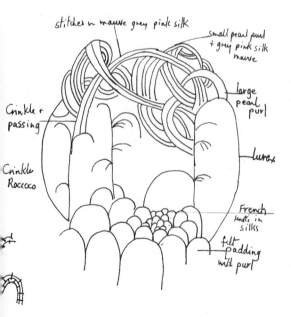

stitches in mauve grey pink silk

small pearl purl
+ grey pink silk
mauve

large
pearl
purl

Crinkle +
passing

Crinkle
Rococo

lurex

French
knots in
silks

felt
padding
with purl

See also colour plate facing page 144

97

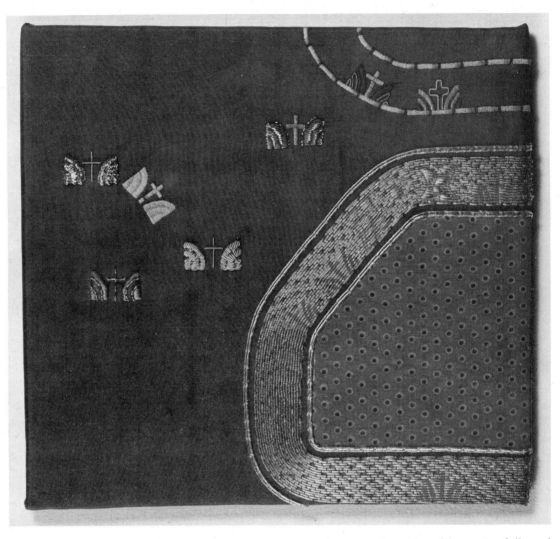

152 A design inspired by drawings of ancient Japanese armour.

The shape at the right of the design in pink voile spotted in brown apricot and white is applied to a grey silk ground. The colours of the spots are repeated in the silk couching stitches which hold the silver threads of the border in place.

The pattern in the border is first tacked out onto the ground, so that this can be followed by the couching row by row.

The small padded areas on the left are tiny repeats of the applied shape and of the border pattern. Silver purl and silk satin stitch cover the padding.

The border outline above the solid silver border is worked in satin stitch in graded colours of pink, brown and green

Gloria Marsh

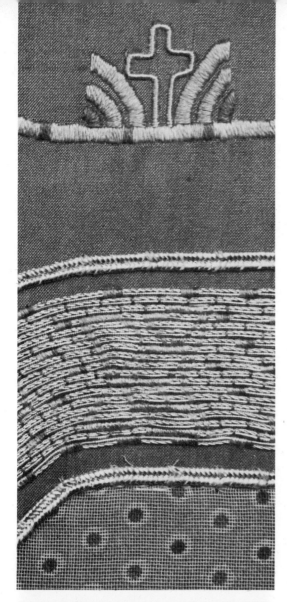

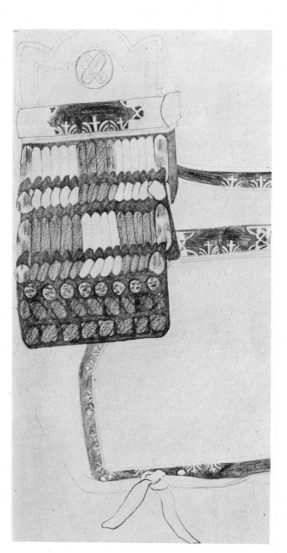

153, 154 Details

155 Original sketch for design

156

157 A design inspired by photographic studies of the surface of a pineapple. (156, 158 and 159) The repetitive shape being treated in different ways.

Worked on a background of brown silk with padded areas of red and yellow shot silk.

The background is first framed up taut with a backing and the design tacked out.

The areas of the design to be padded are cut out in silk considerably larger than the area to be covered. The edges of the silk shape are turned and tacked under, then pleated to fit the area of the design and blind hemmed into place. A space is left open for a soft padding of cotton wool to be inserted, and then closed with the completed hemming. The centre of the area is stitched through to the background to make an indentation.

Other areas of the design are worked in rows of flat couching in a variety of gold threads, and also silk and cotton threads in orange browns and greens. Some centres are padded in felt and covered with purl, and silk and cotton threads. The design is continued to the edge in the same way *Debbie Barclay*

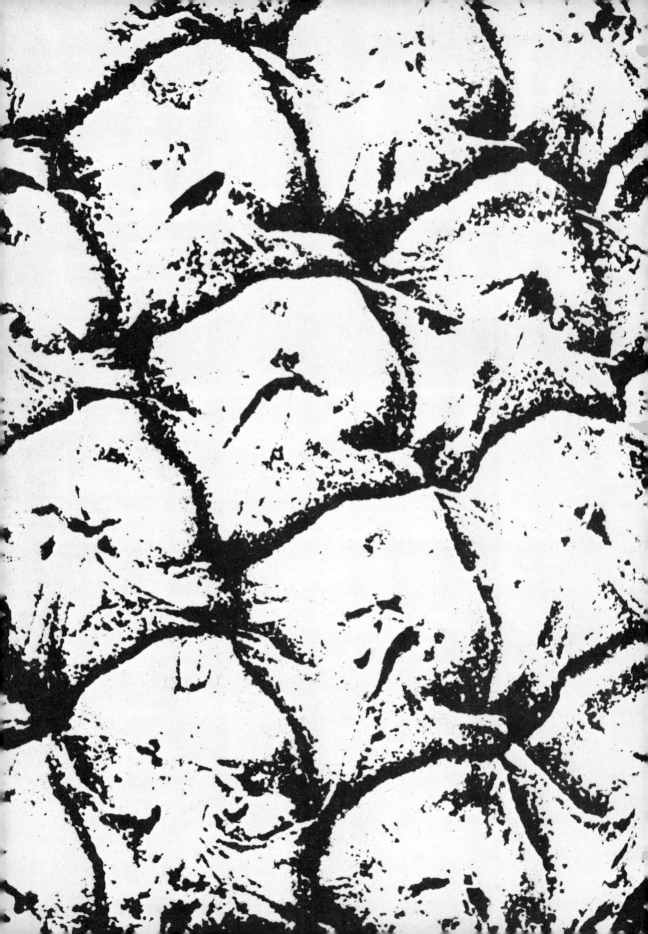

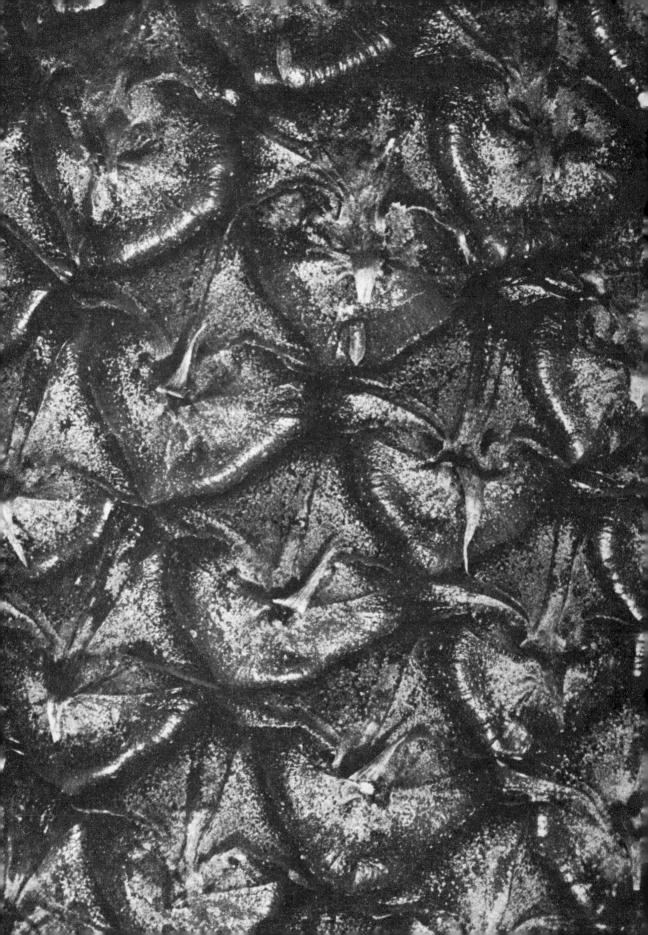

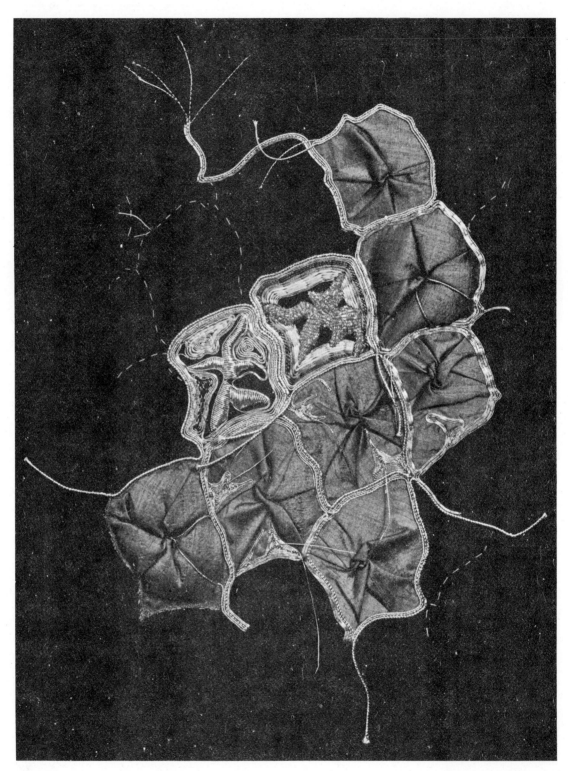

160 Early stage of work on 157.

161 Detail of 157.

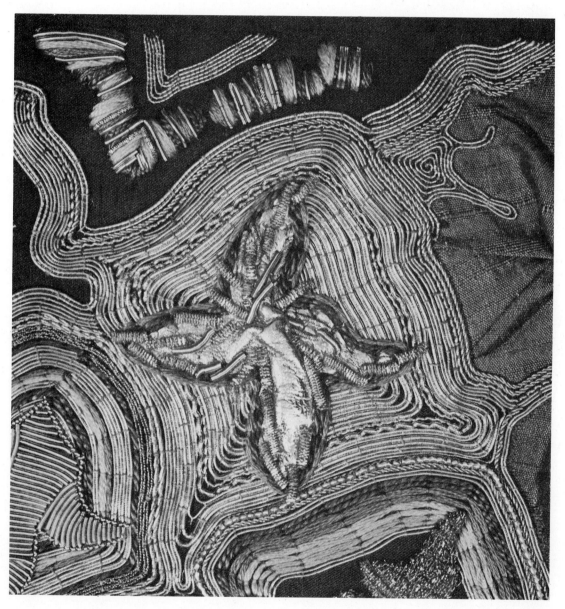

Note two very different but very successful designs both using the construction of one unit of design in different ways.

One design gives an overall repeating pattern boldly and richly, if somewhat crudely, worked. The other is minutely thought out for balance and detail and is finely worked.

163 This dramatic drawing is an obvious inspiration, and it has been sensitively developed into a study of colour and gold textures by the use of burden stitch as in the panel overleaf.

The design is tacked out on a taut background, and gold passing is couched over the area to be filled. Evenly placed silk stitches are then worked over the gold lines varying the colours as required.

Some use of gold over padding accents the design   *Pamela Whatmore*

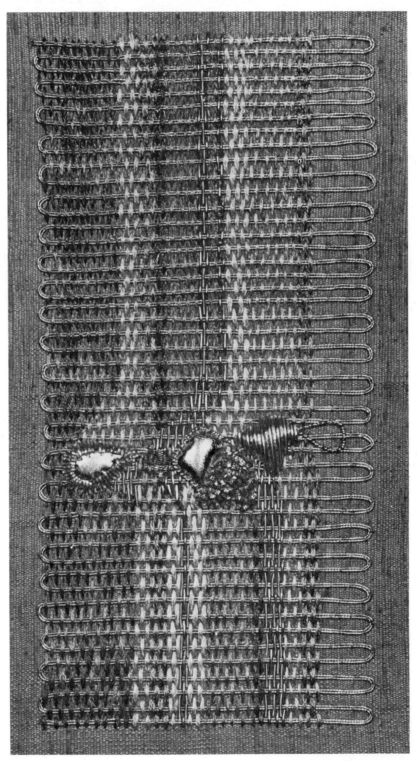

165 Working sketches

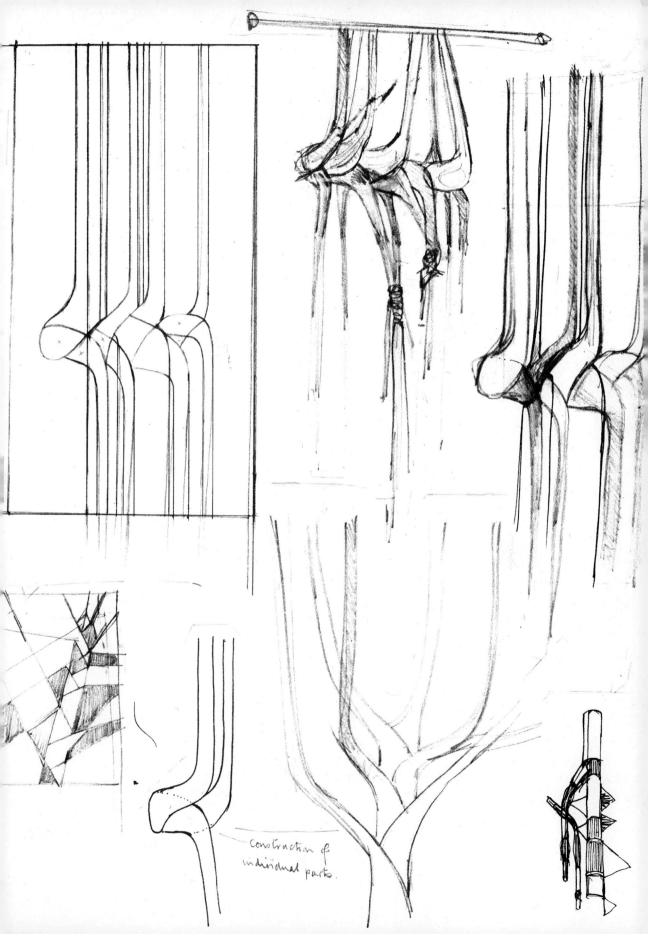

construction of
individual parts.

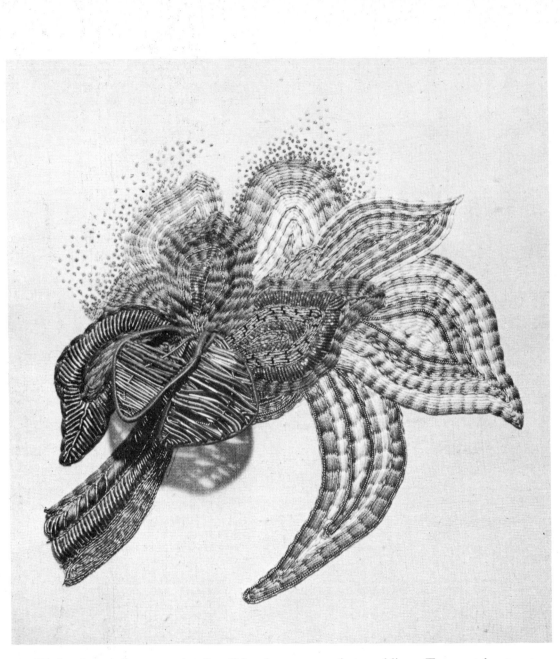

166 Design from museum study of traditional Jacobean flowers.

Worked on a cream silk background, with rows of couched pale brown, cream and green silk and cotton threads, laid alongside various gold threads.

The centre petals are worked in gold purl over string padding. Two petals are constructed of gold wire purl before attaching to the main flower and these petals stand away from the surface embroidery.

French knots and seeding shadow the background to soften the edges and give interest to the somewhat hard outline.

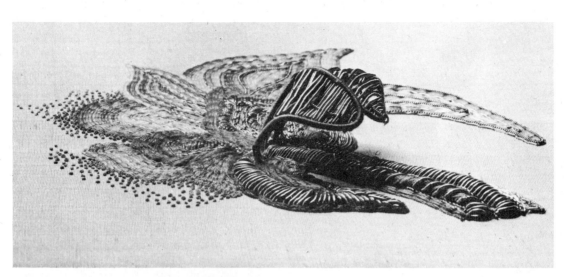

168 Side view showing free-standing petal

167 Detail of outer petals worked first mainly in silk and cotton threads, with outline of centre petals covering the end to make a clear cut finish. The check purl over string can be seen clearly   *Bridget Jones*

169 An experimental and first piece of work introducing padded appliqué, pulled stitches, knotted coral stitch and twisted chain, with gold couching, and purls over padding.

The background is very pale blue evenweave linen, mounted onto frame on a fine linen backing.

The appliqué in matching silk is tacked over a piece of felt, and blind hemmed in place.

The gold threads are couched next, and then the line stitches in self colour. The linen backing is now cut away round the heavy gold work and padding, and pulled stitches are worked to give pattern and texture to the background   *Catherine Muller*

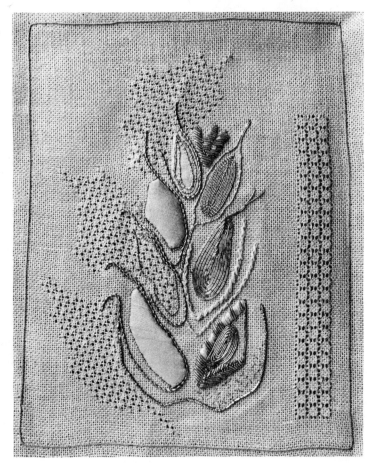

170 Design of shapes working from the natural form of a quartz stone　*Shirley Martin*

171 Design traced out on a brown and bronze shot silk. The applied areas are the reverse side of the ground material, flat and padded, and of both sides of another toning material flat and padded. Padding varies slightly in that applied material is tacked over the last area of felt with the silk edges tacked under. The patch is then sewn in place over the previous layers of felt. Horizontal lines of gold are in place for burden stitch. Another two shapes have been combined for an area gold couching
Shirley Martin

172 The division of the gold couching is marked by a coloured thread. Some shapes are padded with purl, another is seeded and others marked in outline with gold thread

173 A detail shows close seeding of large rough purl, couched twist, rows of soutache and pearl purl. As a first piece of work, it may be noticed, some of the rough purl at the left is cut too short to cover the felt, small pieces of check purl are cut to fill space. French knots also state a shape in self-colour texture

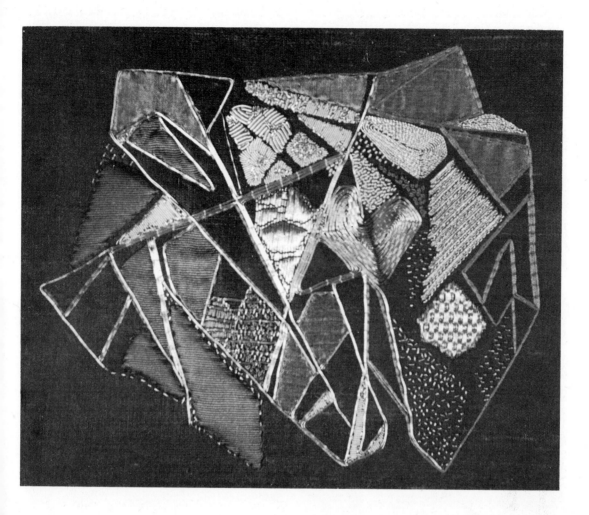

174 The complete design shows tone values working from left to right. Self-coloured areas on left
show as textures, emphasised when necessary by
gold outline, the gold areas to the right are outlined in self and tones of background. A central
gold shape shows card padding still using the same
design element. The heavy shape right is string
padded basket stitch. The light shape left is a
variation of burden in purl

175 Drawing of a popular subject of a cross section of plant form   *Barbara Dawson*

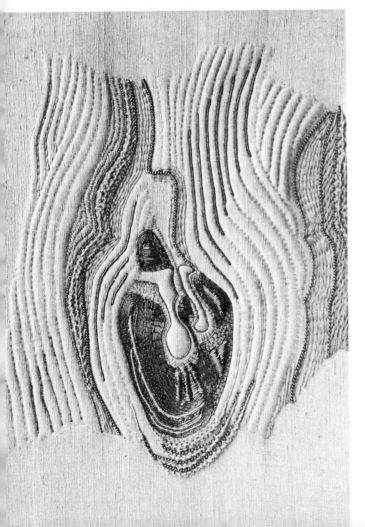

176 A design from a plant cross section worked on ivory coloured silk with a fine rib.

The embroidery includes Italian quilting and line stitches, such as double knot, couching and stem, in wool to tone with background. The wool couching is sewn down with silk thread and gives a glint to the work.

The stitches are all displayed clearly on the background or fitted in between the rows of quilting or in with the gold work.

The gold couching at the centre of the design is accented with a dark brown silk sewing thread. The string padding for the gold couching at the base of the design relates to the ribs of quilting at the side.

The felt padding with purls gives small areas of a different texture from the quilting, gold couching and line stitches.

177, 178 Details

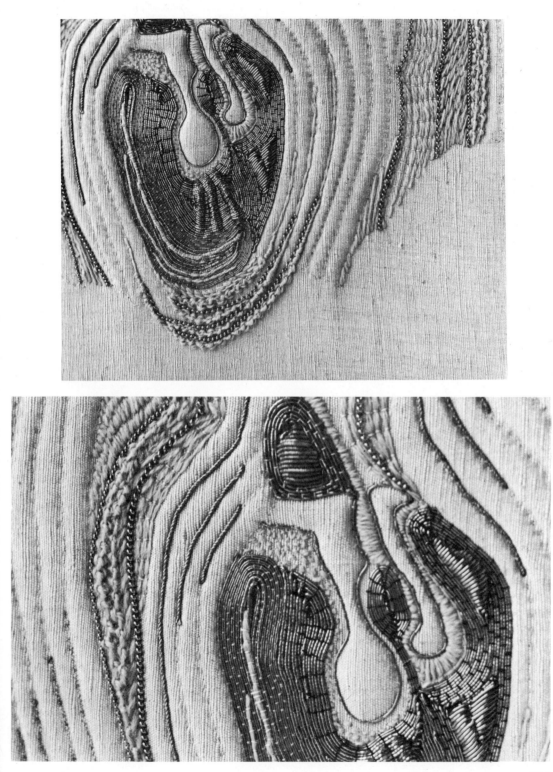

179 Detail from a panel inspired by markings of
tree bark   *Flora Walton*

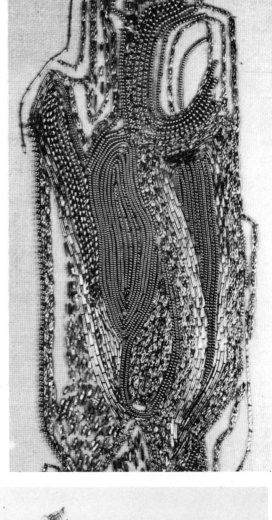

180 Sketch of a tree stump, with strange right
angle shape   *Barbara Dawson*

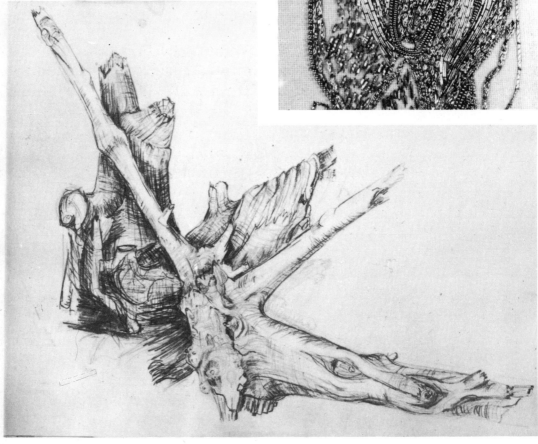

181 An abstract design worked in burden stitch on dark blue silk using brilliant coloured floss silks of magenta, red, light blue, and purple.

A foundation of various gold threads including gold plate twist and passing is couched in place over the design. As the floss silk stitches are worked the ends of the threads are used as a fringe as each row of burden stitch is completed.

The work is mounted on to a large piece of purple silk and then stretched over hard-boards, otherwise the work may be thought of as a flexible free hanging   *Maria Jenkins*

182

183 A simple development of pattern from a drawing of natural form, repeated in different ways such as a solid shape, an outline, the shape divided, placed edge to edge, with a trailing line for contrast

184 An embroidery developed in a similar way, with the addition of background interest. An impression of pattern when looked into reveals a swimming creature. Worked on brown textured with ochre, furnishing material

Marjorie Thomson

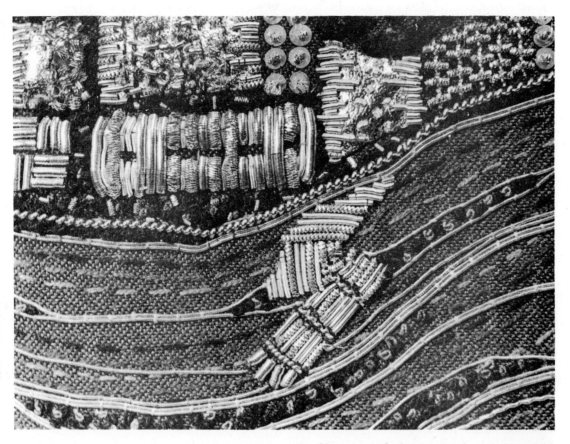

185 Shows use of spangles, burden stitch at right and seeded purls with french knots

186 Design from studies and sketches of landscape.

The background is of two printed cottons of even tone, one in brown printed blue, the other in two tones of brown. The print is used in the design where the fine tambour thread is worked more closely over the flowers of the print.

Basic methods of goldwork in a variety of threads used with felt and string padding interpret the design richly. The tambour thread in the background suggests a soft atmosphere and is a setting for the heavier work at the centre *Pam Whatmore*

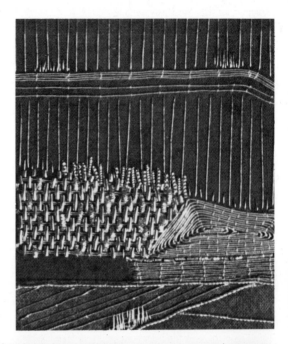

187 Detail

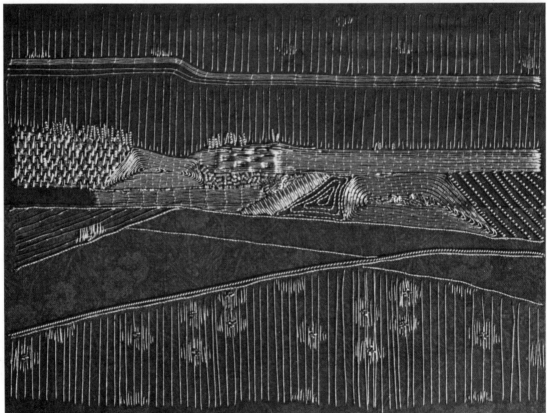

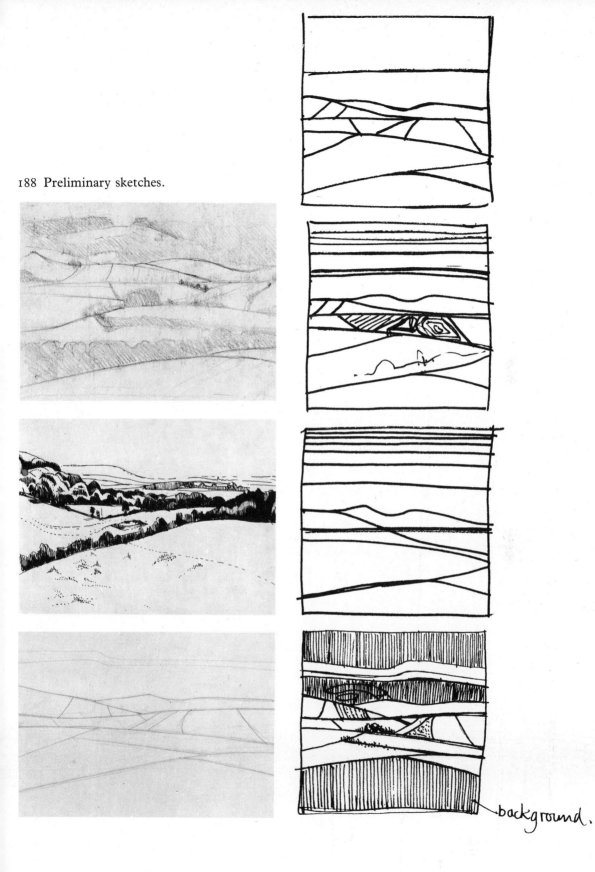

188 Preliminary sketches.

background.

189 A rich interpretation, with a peasant atmosphere, of a country scene worked on welsh flannel in stripes of three tones of green: dark green behind the gate, mid, and light for the sky.

The centre shows a field with rows of different treatments of couched gold, using silk and cotton threads in blue and green. The top of the design shows a pattern of fields and sky which links with the crossbars of the gate at the bottom.

The crossbars are worked in gold purl and red silk over string padding, the leaves in gold purl over felt padding, and stalks and twigs in gold pearl purl   *Julia Sorrell*

190, 191   Details

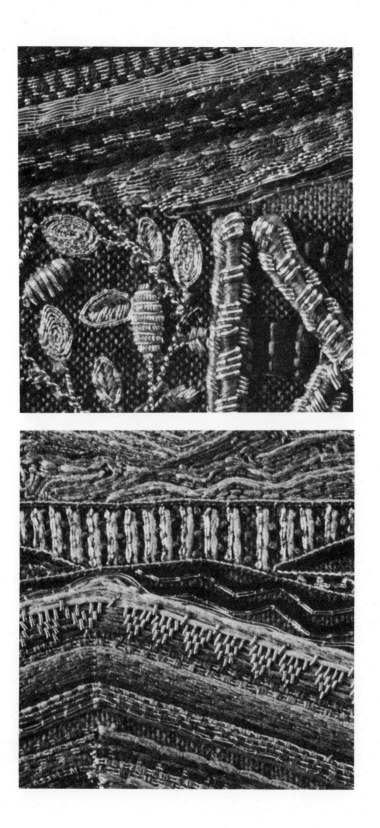

192 A design giving an appearance of upward growth worked on an evenly woven welsh flannel in a formalised style of blackwork.

The patterns in the blocks at the top of the design are worked on a grid of laid gold passing, as in traditional blackwork patterns.

At the base of the design, the patterns are arranged in rows to give border designs

Lorraine Bathgate

193 A design developed from a curved line into a dream landscape. The continuous curved line displays the shine of the gold and silver threads couched side by side on a brilliant blue silk background. A break is made in the smooth threads by basketwork over string padding. Highly coloured silks are used to embroider trees and plant-like shapes, to give a gay and lively result

Marion Kite

194 Detail

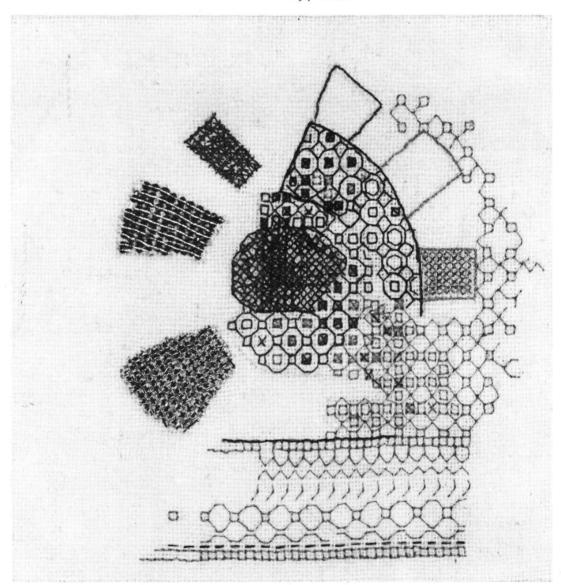

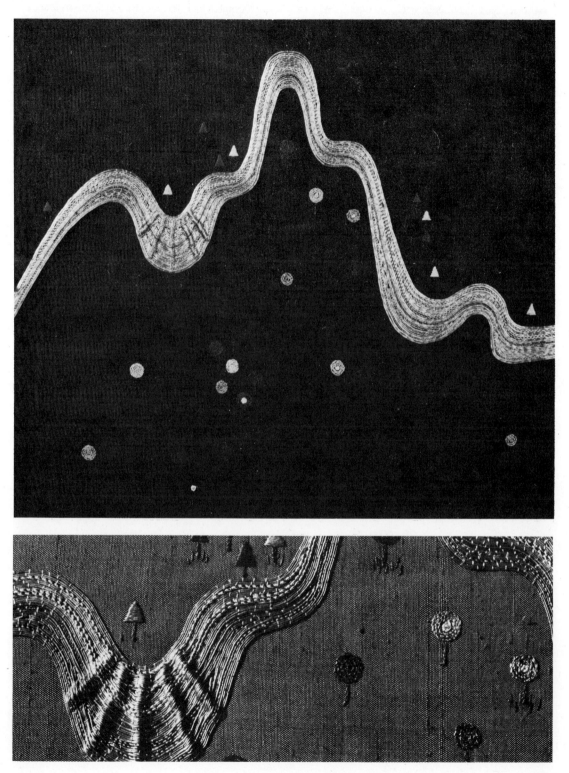

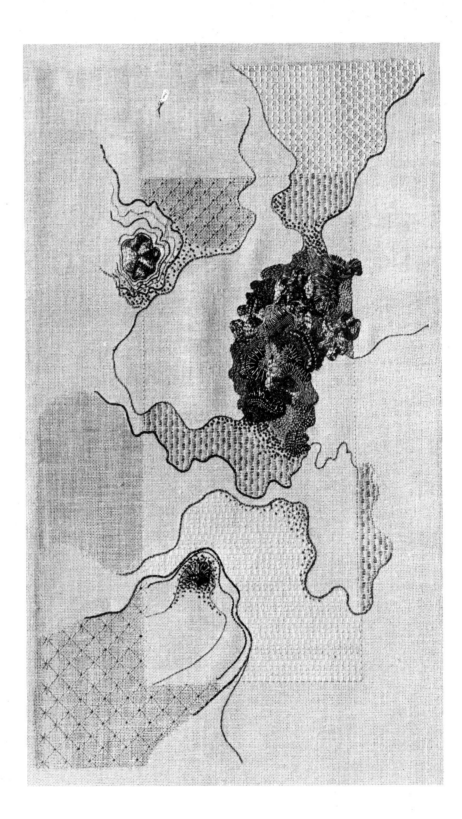

195 A design developed from curved lines, and showing interesting solid areas of embroidery, combining gold work pulled stitches and line stitches.

Worked on an even weave linen, the material is mounted in a frame on a backing, and the design is tacked out on a taut frame.

The metal threads are then worked and include couched gold, flat and over padding, gold purls combined with natural coloured silk threads. Meticulously worked chain, stem, back and run stitches set off the accuracy of the gold work.

To work the pulled stitches on the background, the backing is cut away from this area, while the work is still in the frame.

The pulled stitches and some counted patterns are then worked.

The change from very solid work to near transparency and the fine execution make a satisfying piece of craftsmanship

Marion Kite

196 Detail of top left

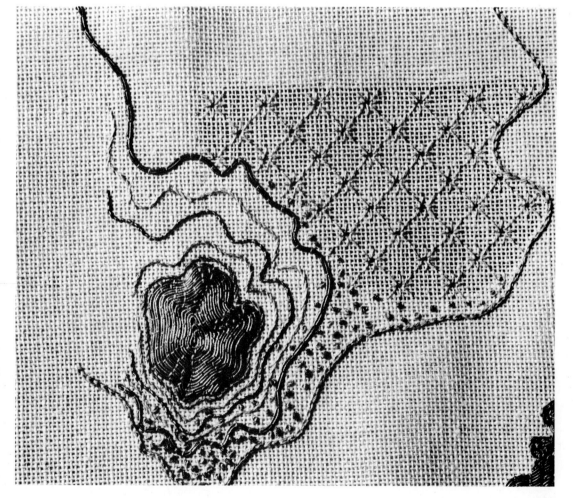

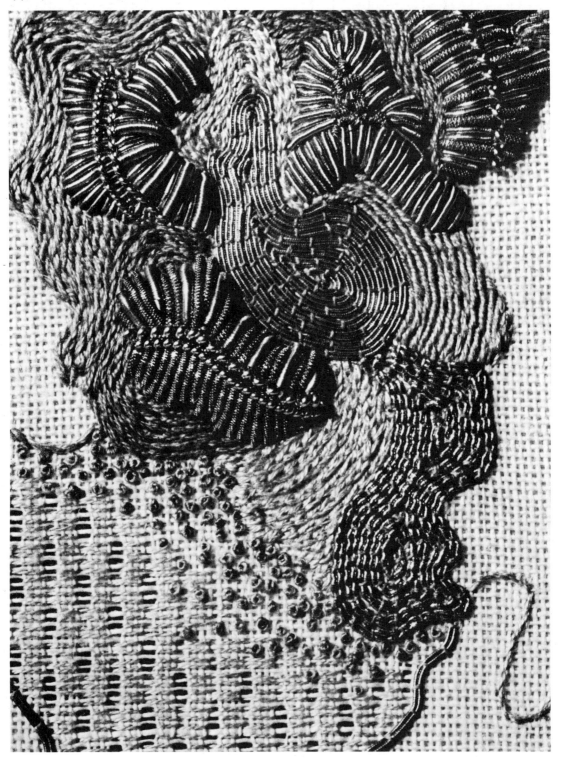

199 A design from a landscape interpreted by curving lines used in outline for the trees and clouds interlacing for the hills and streams, and as circles for the flowers. Straight lines for stems stabilise the design.

Worked on a lightweight wool and cotton mixture in yellow green, dark green and mauve.

The appliqué for the two-colour background is prepared first and mounted with a backing on a frame. The design is then tacked out on a taut frame.

The appliqué for the trees is cut out from the working drawing, and applied to the design.

The metal threads are couched in brick stitch and radiating lines, and in some areas over string padding to give a rippled pattern.

The metal threads used are twist, passing, imitation jap and antique gold. Mauve and green cotton are also used for couching alongside the gold.

Rows of floss silk outline the tree and shows highlights similar to metal thread.

The picture frame has a surround of gold lamé and a narrow edge of dark green wood supports the glass   *Irene Ord*

200 Abstract treatment of landscape, working from straight rows of strata giving way to an erupting curve.

Organised tying down stitches make a constructive pattern and are developed into part of the design, in satin stitch blocks graded along the base   *Rosalind McClinton*

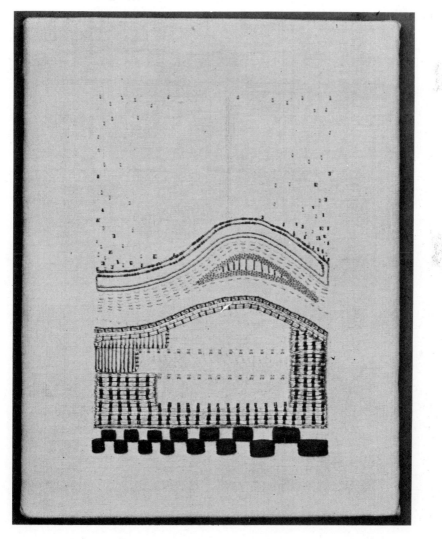

201 Design inspired by drawings of costume garments.

The corset forms a design of curving lines of differing emphasis.

Worked on a background of aubergine-coloured cotton printed with black flowers, parts of the design are applied in beige silk and pale pink satin.

The background material is framed up with a backing and the design tacked out.

The design is also tacked out in sections on the appropriate material to be applied. The embroidered lines in hand and machine and the Italian quilting are worked. The edges of the applied areas are turned under and tacked, then blind hemmed into position matching the tack lines of the design.

The metal threads are couched in place with a coloured thread to tone with the background and the appliqué. Extra colour is given by adding a thread of silk with the metal threads to be couched.

The couching stitches are sometimes arranged to form a pattern of flowers similar to the background. The pattern is tacked out on the area of background to be covered, and followed row by row by the couching stitch. Other flowers are marked in satin stitch in beige, pink and aubergine coloured silk.

Machine stitching in dark thread and Italian
202 Machine stitching in dark thread and Italian quilting. The different metal threads can be identified, and can be seen to shade from dark to light with the silk threads between.
203 The pattern worked in couching over the gold twist border worked on pink satin. The area on the left is beige silk with hand couched lines   *Marion Gilling-Baker*

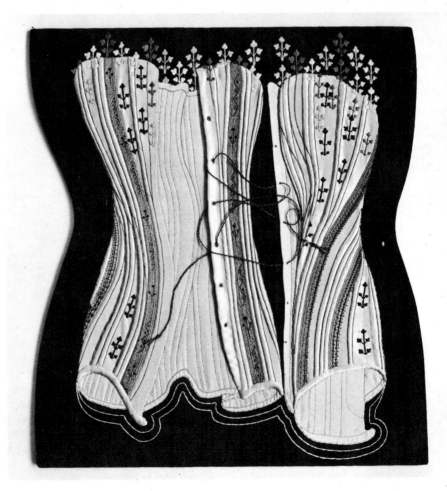

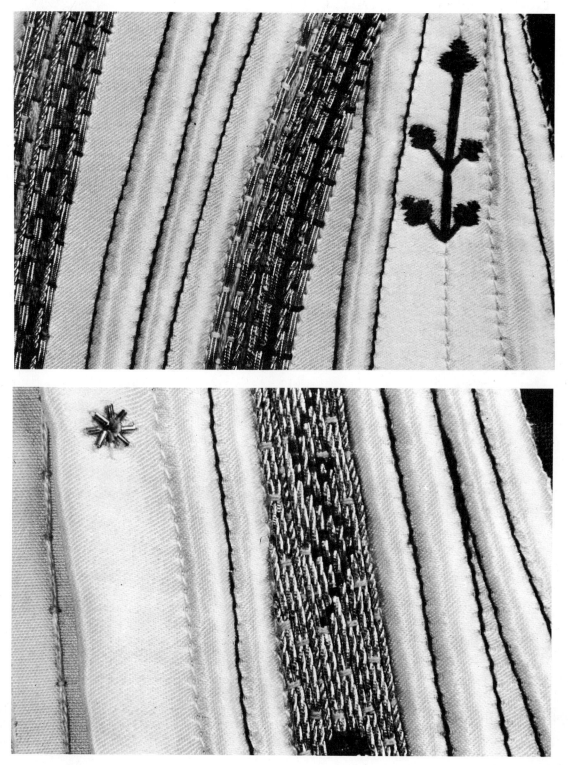

204

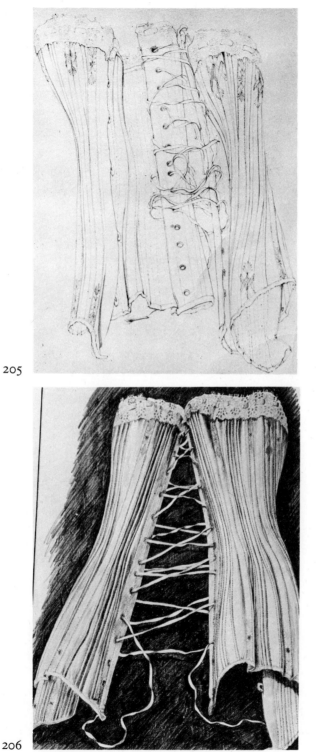

205

206

207-8 Life drawings and studies are a preparation for all figure work   *Diane Bates*

209-10 Sketch designs for *Adam and Eve* panel
Josie Barnes

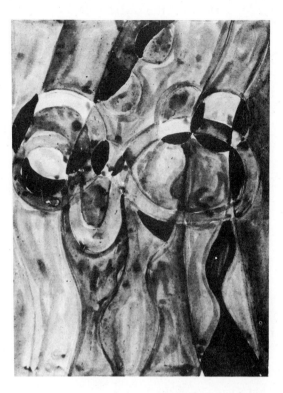

211 Developments into study of curving lines and broken circles

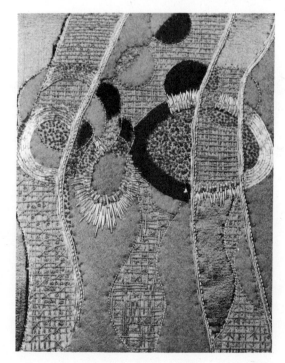

212 Completed panel executed in appliqué felt, velvet shot silk with laid patterns. Jap gold couching and restrained use of passing and crinkle and purls and string combine to make an original embroidery

213 A design of 'Kissing Couples' worked on taupe silk satin in various metal threads such as copper, silk, antique silver and gold.

The threads are mixed and couched using rows of silver next to copper, and copper with gold. This gives a pink hue to the gold and silver, and other nuances as the mixing is varied. Padding with purls is also used

Anne Gillespie

See also colour plate facing page 145

214 Preliminary sketch of 'Kissing Couples' design

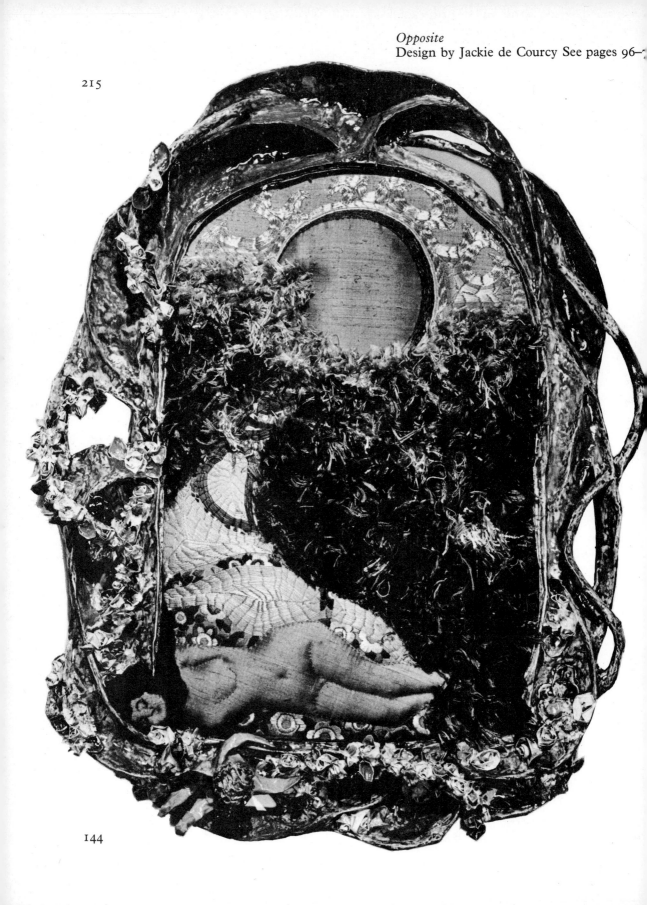

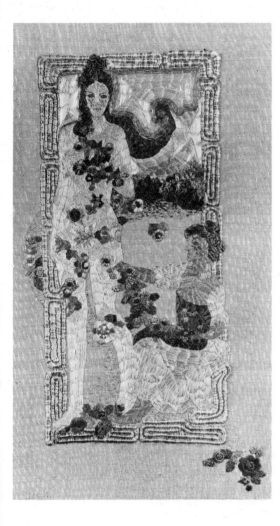

215–7 Three different expressions of pastoral scenes of nymphs.

This work displays how very simple use of gold thread can add richness to a design, and the similarity of how the shine of floss silks varies in the same way as metal thread.

216 Shows couched metal thread in the padded border
215 Shows purl loosely worked into a tufted background, and couched gold at the top of the design. The papier-maché frame shows a personally-created setting   *Margaret Hall*

Opposite:
Kissing Couples Anne Gillespie See pages 142–3

217 Shows couched metal thread in the background

218 Detail of 219

219 Design from a tatoo inspired by circus and pop festivals, and worked on white cotton with red and blue flowers; the leg is tan coloured cotton appliqué. The lady with a serpent is mounted on a dagger entwined with a motto. Gold kid over padded felt makes a strong statement for the dagger. Red and blue silk are used for the motto. The other figure is outlined in gold passing *Sue White*

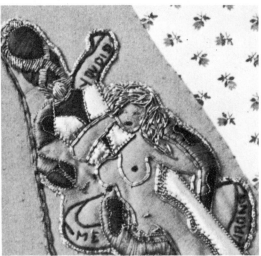

146

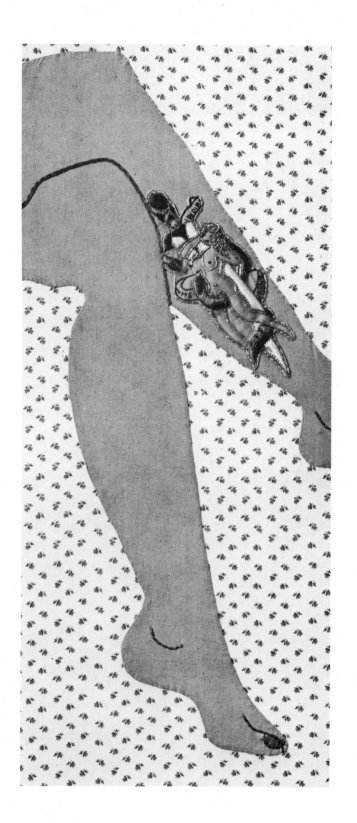

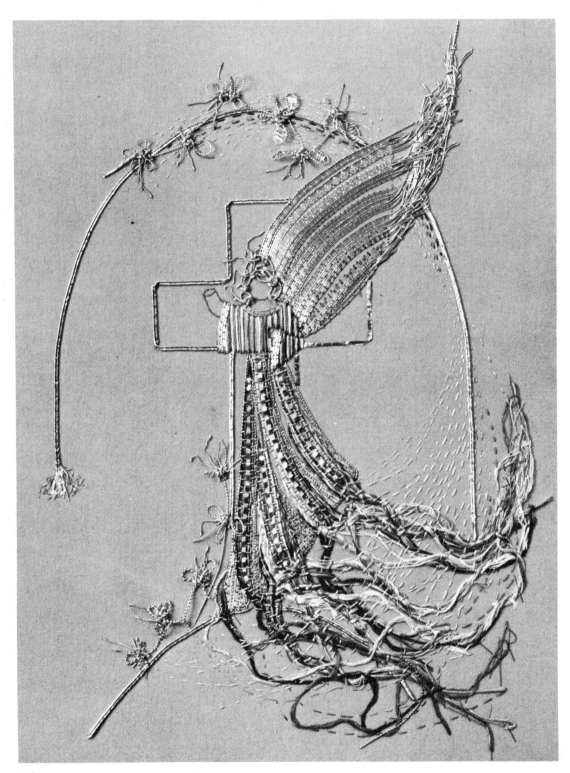

221 Detail of dress

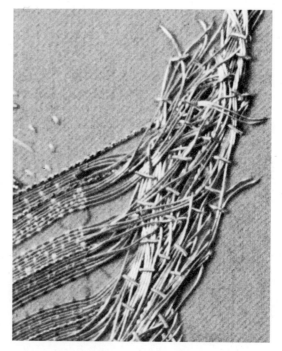

222 Detail of wing

220 A design of a Guardian Angel from drawings of tomb stones. A curving line from the tip of the wing to the hem of the robe sweeps across the rectangle.

Worked on flame coloured lightweight wool, the couching on the wing is very finely worked in spectrum colours. Couching stitches form small repeating patterns on the wing, where the ends of the gold threads are freely arranged and sewn in place with gold purls.

The robe is worked in silk laid threads in rainbow colours, with gold plate, twist and purl added in sections to the skirt.

The ends of the silk laid threads are held in place with running stitches and balance with the wing.

The encircling gold line behind the figure is decorated with free standing flowers of gold pearl purl and smooth purl   *Jane Denyer*

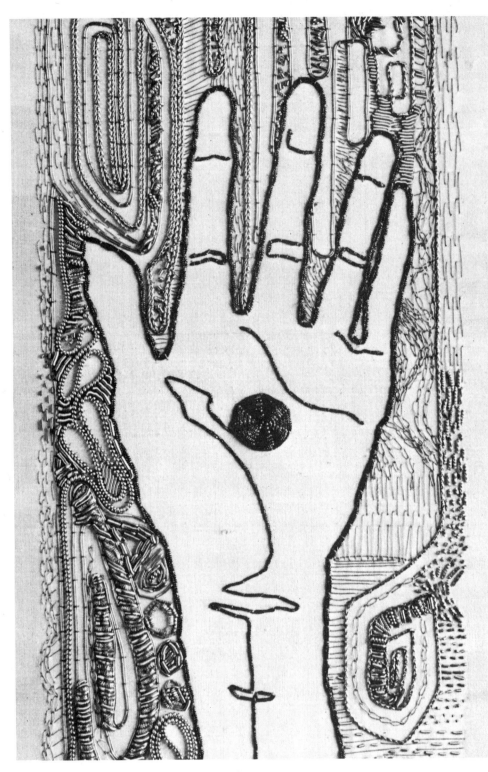

223 Design for a burse on a white silk background. The crucified Hand is outlined in a dark green or antique metal thread, and the patterns of the wood behind the Hand is worked in different types of gold, including chain stitch in tambour gold, purl over string, couched passing, twist, and graded purls used as a filling   *Judy Bury*

224 An experiment, combining silver thread and quilting. Worked on grey silk, the design is taken from an American grave stone
                    Joan Ramsden

225 A hanging of natural raw silk showing an abstract design with an applied purple triangle of silk, worked into the background with curving lines of gold thread and purple silk.

Gold purls over felt padding contrast with large areas of flat couched gold threads. Shadows of the padded shapes are worked in purple silk to show through the couched area, as in *or nué*　　　*Marion Kite*

226 Detail

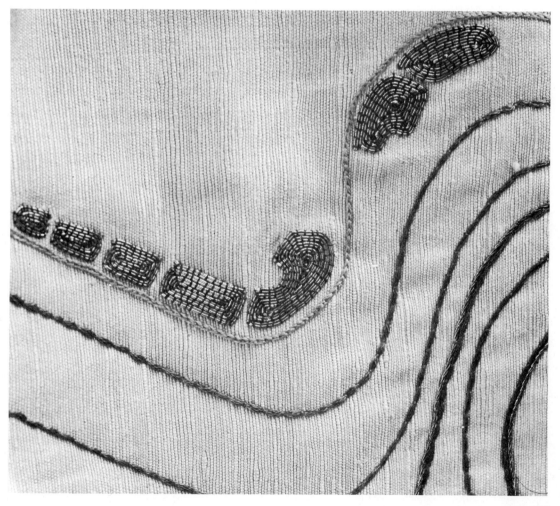

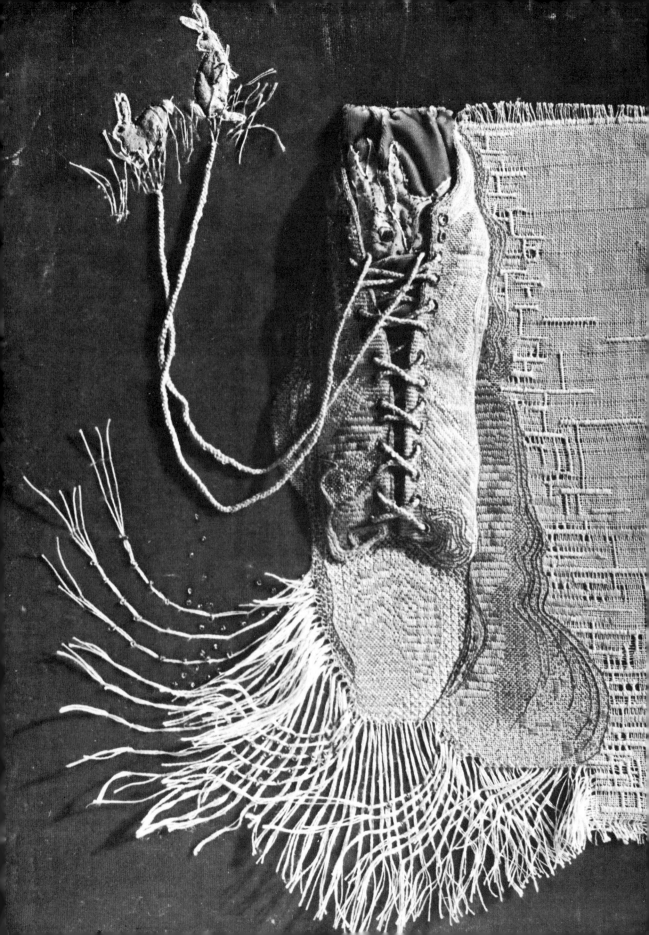

227 Design from studies of shoes, given a personal interpretation in combining padding, pulled stitches and counted thread patterns. Worked in stranded cottons and fine gold thread.

The counted thread work on evenweave linen is worked first and applied onto a soft green velvet background. The design appears to grow out of the background. Purls tie down some of the frayed edges of the linen

Mandy Levy

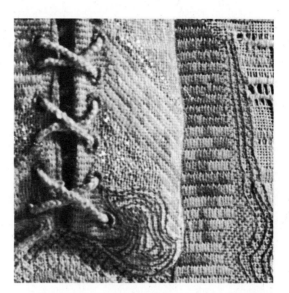

228 Detail

229 Sketch of a shoe

230 Further sketches

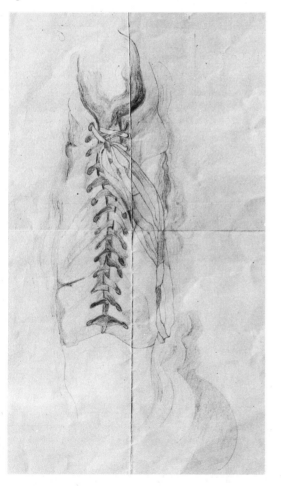

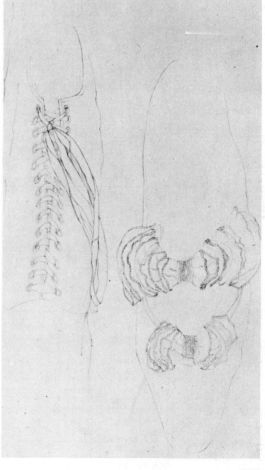

231 Drawing of painted jar

232 A simple design from a painted jar with use of shadows to form different background textures. Worked on purple satin backed silk, with russet velvet appliqué.

The design is prepared in the usual way with a working drawing of the main outlines. The background is mounted into an em-

broidery frame with a backing, and the design tacked out through tracing paper.

Silver couching for the jar is worked first and where the floral pattern occurs close couching stitches in different colours cover the silver row by row.

The velvet area is cut to shape, and the edge turned under and slip hemmed in place.

234 The padded silk area is prepared as in the diagram. The smallest piece of felt is laid first and the largest last so making a smooth surface. The last piece of felt is covered with purple silk cut from the template with turnings allowed for folding over the edge of felt. The silk-covered felt is then blind hemmed into place.

Note needles are used as pins as these mark the material less than pins.

The area between the velvet appliqué and the padded silk shape is filled with silver couching.

Note the accuracy of the bricking of the couching stitches round the curved areas.

The opposite side of the background is decorated with a pattern of burden stitch selectively arranged and shaded in purple and copper silk next to the edge of the jar

Jane Iles

236 A hanging designed for a composite embroidery, having a Chinese influence, and worked on a natural silk background.

A feature is the couched gold in curving lines supported by other areas of gold couching in various threads, held in place by white silk in a pattern of scallops.

Machine whip stitch is worked in tones of blue-green in the form of scallops to make a solid filling. The machine embroidery is worked first and completed and then applied to the main design.

Laid fillings and cross stitch in silk thread form a powdered filling of grey and blue and red working the colours together and sometimes mixed, i.e. red upright crossed by blue horizontal.

Curving lines of chain stitch in two tones of blue follow the design and take it over the edge of the silk background onto the mount of the hanging which is in silk Noiles, and matches the silk of the embroidered background but of a different texture.

Other embroidery may be identified as satin stitch in graded tones of neutral silks, fine seeding and french knots

Susan Rigg Kemp

237 Detail

238 Design from studies of gardens. The gateway arch is used again as posts for tubs. Experimentally worked gold thread can be seen in the tree, flowers, and gate, which, together with the treatment of shrubs shows obvious enjoyment worked on cream silk ground   *Ksynia Marko*

239–41 Details

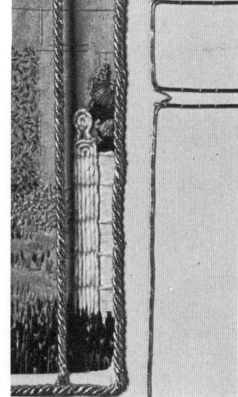

242 A design taken from a Victorian doorway, worked on stone coloured satin.

The careful planning of the mitres at the corners of the door panels makes a feature of the gold couching at the centre of the design. The use of gold plate surrounding these panels makes a strong contrast of texture.

The angles of the mitred corners are repeated in the arch, as triangles of purl over padded felt.

The pillars of the doorway are of large size purl over thick string and the arch is worked in a smaller size purl over a thin string

Gwen Hart

243 Detail

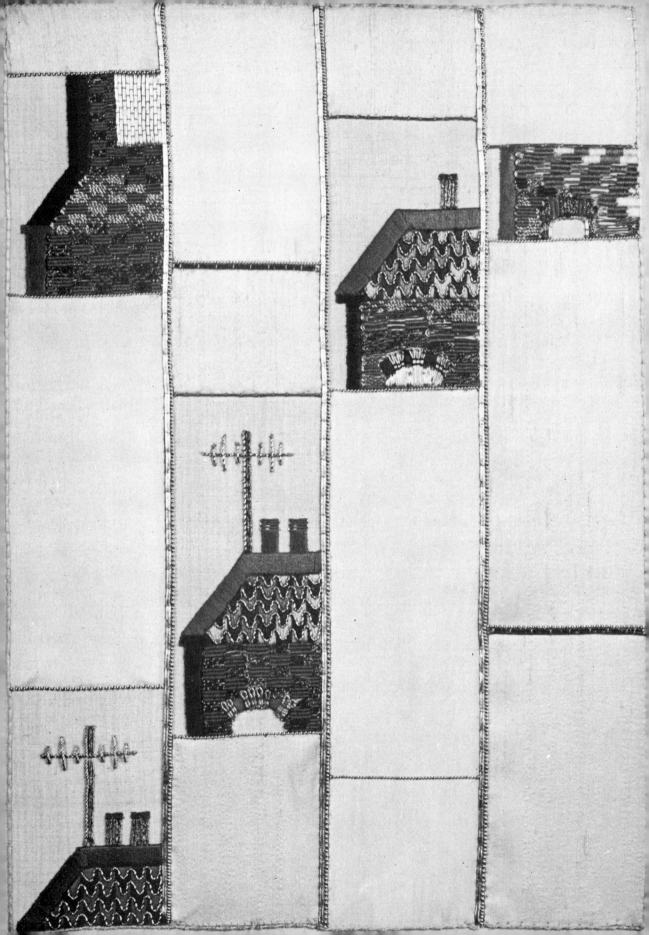

244 A design using houses as a unit for a vertical repeating pattern.

Worked on a background of coarse wild silk with sections of fine silk appliqué in beige and pink silk.

The houses are worked in individually designed fillings, and consist of couching in red silk over a variety of gold metal threads. Different features are accentuated in each section, and show satin stitch in shades of brown, grey and dull green silk thread. Divisions of the background are marked out in pearl purl and passing which set off the different textures of threads. There are many details to study in this work

Caroline Richardson

246 Design from the interior of the Festival Hall, South Bank, London.

Worked on an azure blue silk ground, in silver passing and purls over felt padding.

The feeling of recession of the hall is given by shaded couching stitches.

White floss silk is couched down with the silver passing. Antique-type silver thread is used to set off the theatre boxes, which are padded as in the detail. Note the use of the ring frame *Barbara Dawson*

247 Detail
248, 249 Preliminary sketches

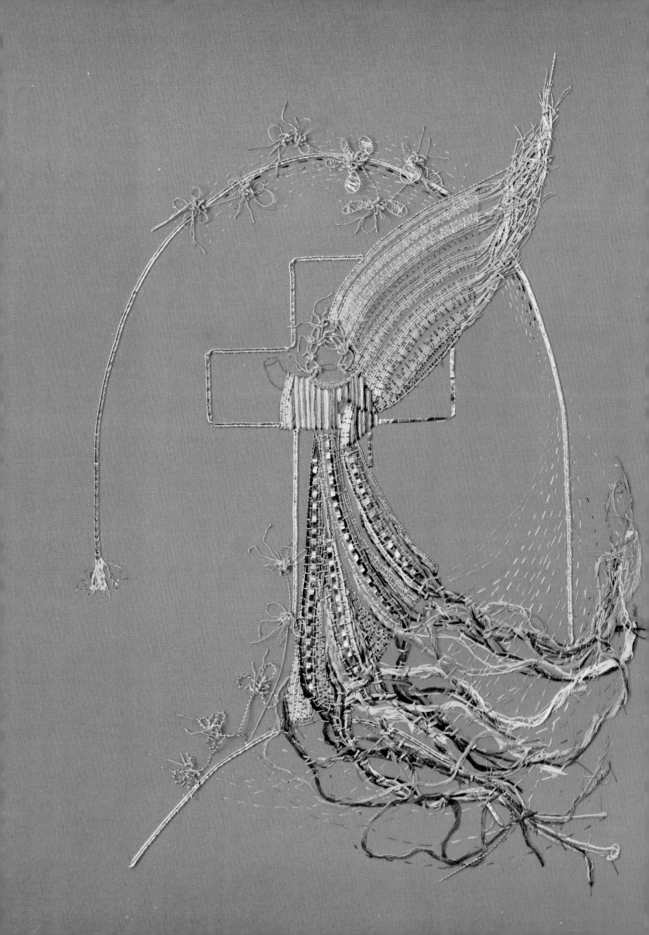

Opposite Guardian Angel Jane Denyer see pages 148–9

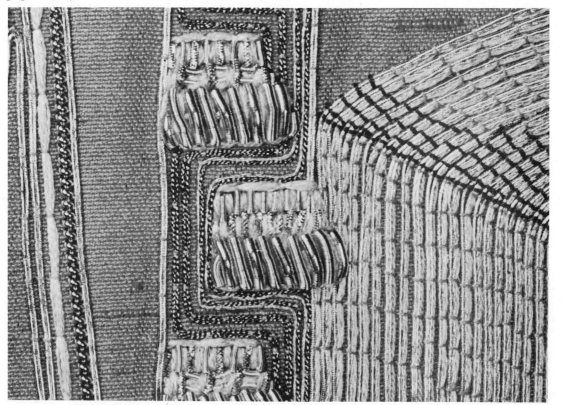

247 Detail of 246 by Celia Goodrick-Clarke

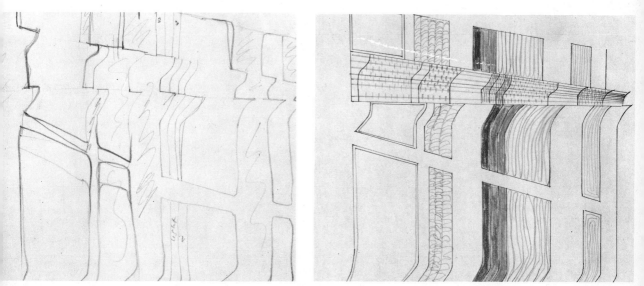

248, 249 Preliminary sketches for 250

250 Design inspired by a beam of light cutting through a window.

Worked on white silk with a block of silk couching in primary colours, red, blue and yellow.

The block of gold plate is closely laid and couched in place next to the silk couching. The plate is crimped on one edge, and a single row of imitation jap is couched in-between.

Other areas are filled with rows of string padding covered with rough, smooth and check purl. (Cover one piece of string before laying the next.)

The horizontal lines are worked in a form of burden stitch.

The outline of the rectangle, lower left, shows a good example of sharp corners and angles *Celia Goodrick-Clarke*

251 and 252 Opposite Details

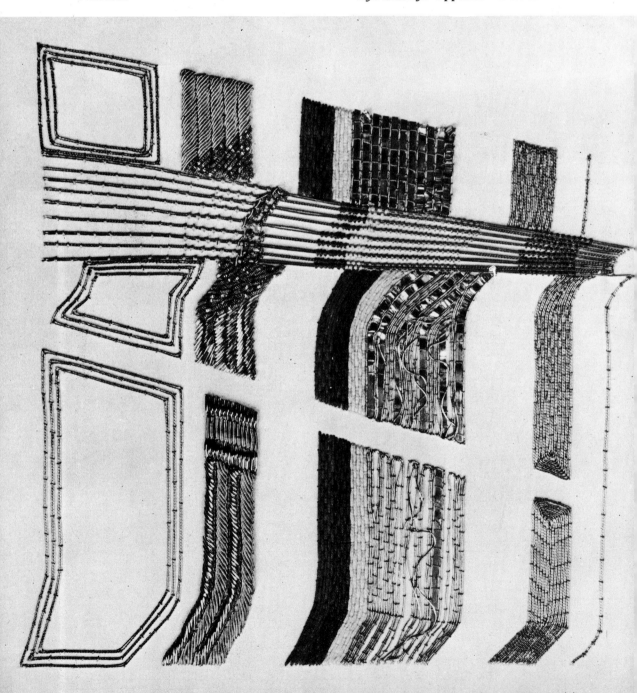

253 A design developed from zigzag lines and points. On the right-hand side the design is simply marked out in passing grading from single to heavier threads. The spaces between are quilted to add richness to support the concentration of heavy gold threads worked on the left. String is used as a padding for the mixed threads which are rolled into a curl at the left. Heavy gold cord is sewn in place as a filling at the base of the design

Celia Goodric Clark

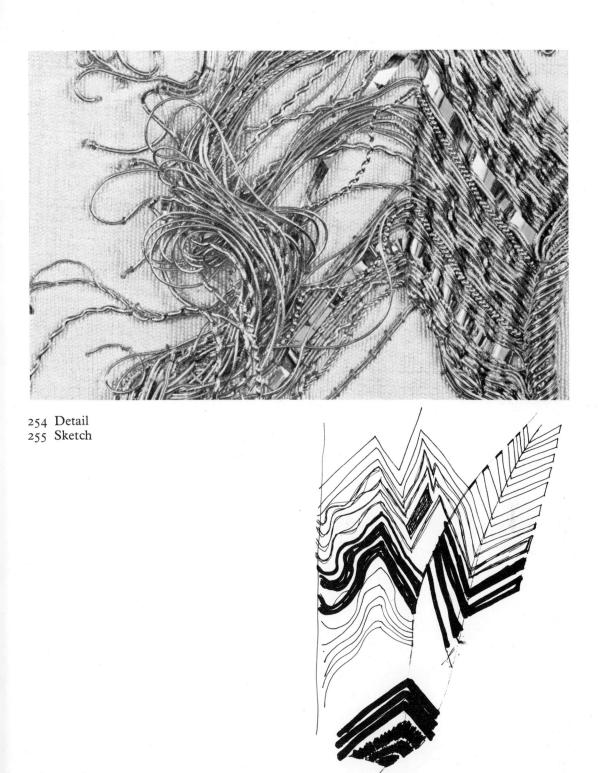

254 Detail
255 Sketch

173

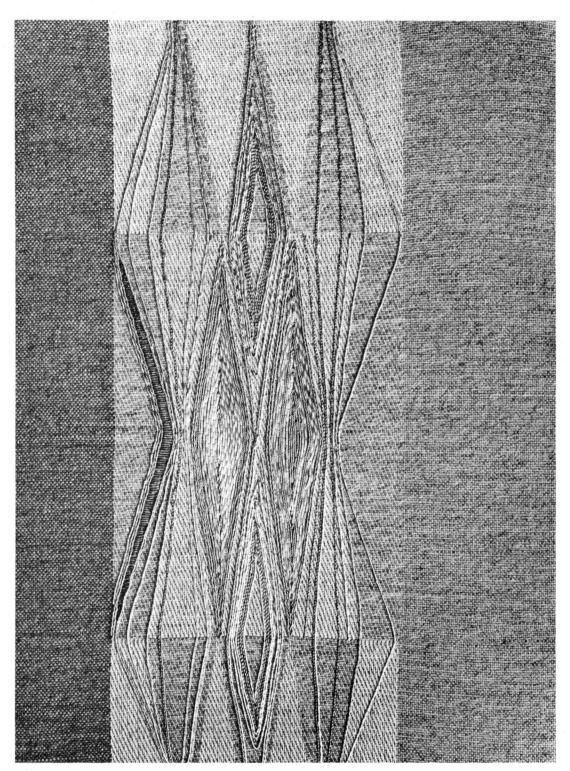

174

256 A geometrical design based on the pattern woven into the background material.

Various metal threads are used in varying thicknesses and density.

A feature is made of by using purls in one area only   *Flora Walton*

258 A design changing from abstract zigzag lines through curving lines to form a feather.

Worked on pale brown silk in single threads of gold and silver together with some neutral silk threads, and finely couched in place.

There is a change of tone with the fall of light on the different angles of the thread
Christine O'Connell

257 Sketch

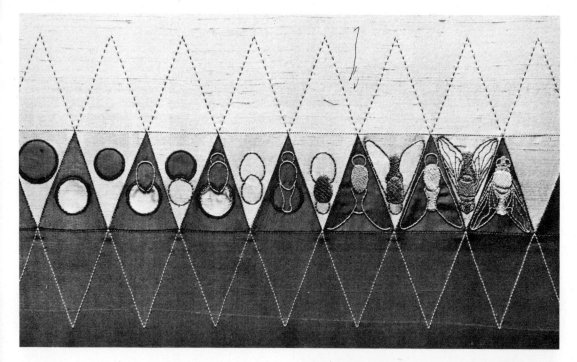

259 Design for a panel, composed of a repeating pattern using badgers as a motif. Worked on grey denim and in gold passing outline, with black and white silk details
Judy Bury

260 A design moving from a row of interlocking triangles to a scarab, showing the abstract circle turn to a natural form.

Worked on a pale mauve shot silk and a red shot with green to give a copper colour.

The embroidery is worked in silver on the mauve and copper threads on the copper silk, using couching and padding covered with purl.

The outlines of the triangles are run stitched on the mauve silk and back stitched on the copper   *Christine O'Connell*

261 Detail

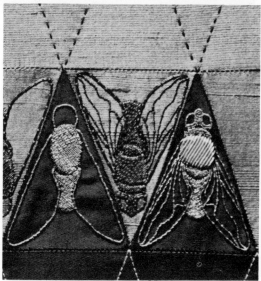

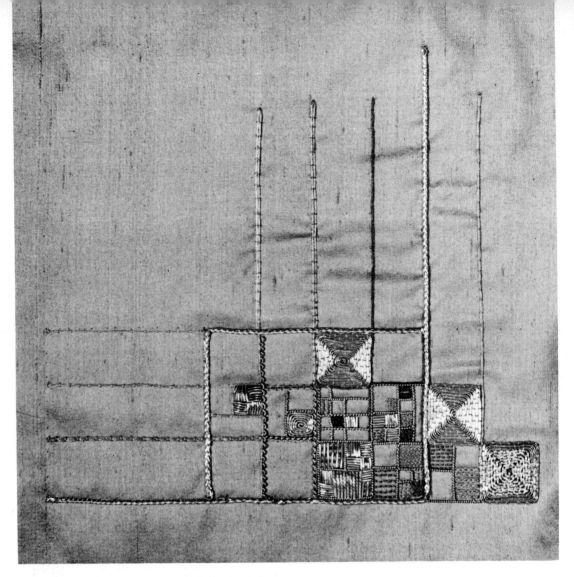

262 A simple and successful start for a design of squares, formed by a grid of horizontal and vertical lines crossing one another.

Worked on pale mauve shot silk, the squares are filled with a variety of methods including couched silver passing, silver twist and crinkle threads, and silver purl over felt padding.

Grey, mauve, blue and pink silk and cotton threads are used for couching down the metal threads to give colour to the silver, and are also laid with silver.

Chain and back stitches and french knots are used to fill some of the divisions of the squares.

Note the change of tone as the light falls on different sides of the squares   *Sue Moss*

264 Work in good condition when removed from frame

263 Detail

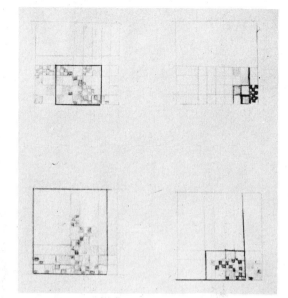

265 Sketches

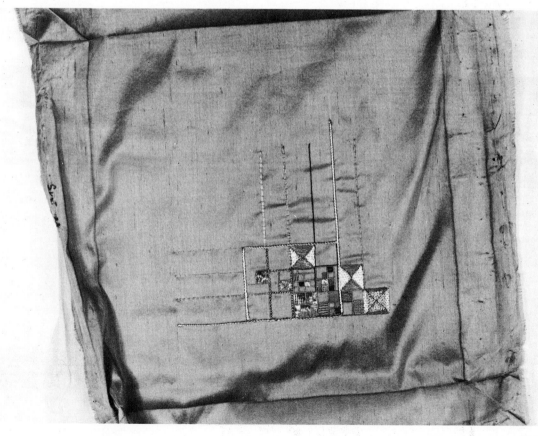

266 A design from drawings of string tied to a grid and studies of curved and straight lines.

Worked on a gold coloured silk background and finely couched in gold with stitches of pink silk. The silk stitches are worked closely together to give shadows on the gold. In other areas the design is worked in pink silk couched down with self stitches, or fine stem stitch

Christine O'Connell

267, 268 Details

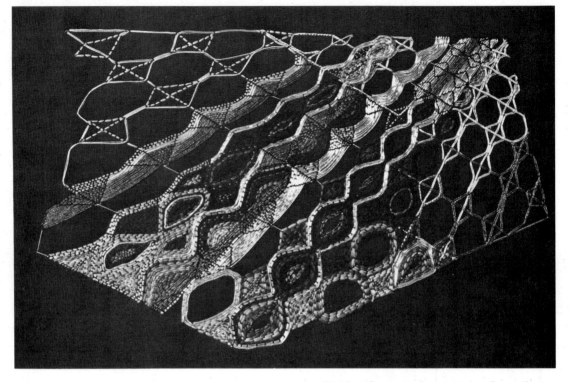

269 Design from a photograph of a grille or grid, taken from an angle giving a floating and gradated appearance.

Worked on dark green and black raw silk, different parts of the grid are accentuated by couching in different coloured silk cotton and gold threads. The colours of similar tone to the background are blue, brown, red and green, and blend with dark antique golds to make a very rich piece of work.

The couching stitches vary in colour and spacing, some being very close together, and this shades and colours the gold and silk threads as well as making a pattern and becomes a simple example of *or nué* or shaded gold *Danena Wrightson-Hunt*

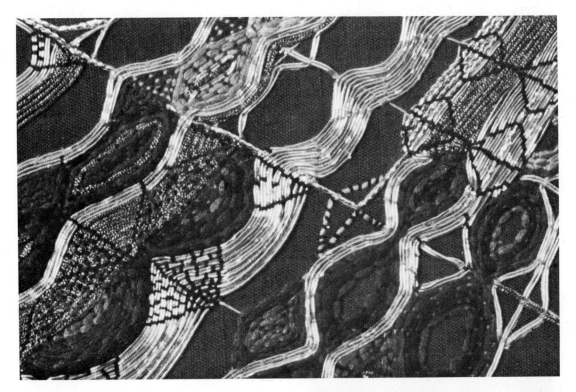

270 Detail
271 Original inspiration for the design

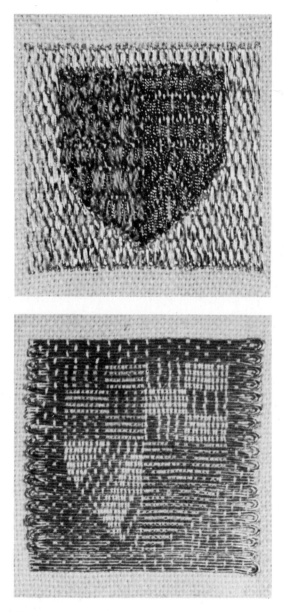

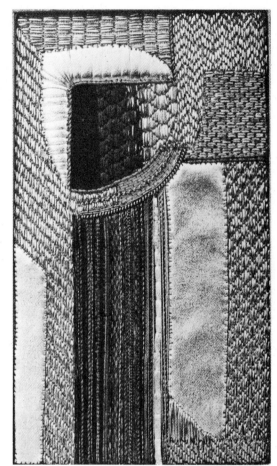

Shields
272 Method of underside couching
273 Method of *or nué* otherwise known as
Italian shading or shaded gold

274 A design by Judith Summers inspired by engineering and, except for the areas of gold kid, worked entirely in couche rentre, or underside couching. This method, typical of the work by hand in early *Opus Anglicanum*, fell out of use because it required meticulous skill and considerable time, and was replaced by the now familiar method of couching. For couche rentre (re-entered couching) on evenly woven linen scrim, which allowed careful counting, was used mounted on a linen back of a closer weave. Working on the top side of frame, the metal thread is a fine pliable machine thread in gold or silver, and is sewn down in maltese silk by bringing the couching thread up in the background over the metal thread and returning in exactly the same position carefully nipping or pulling a minute loop of metal through to the underside. The couching thread is drawn into place and brought up to the top surface approximately four threads of the linen from the first position. A complete row is worked in this way. The stitches of the next row are placed exactly adjacent for a barred pattern at the top left, one thread down from the position of the first row, as in darning, for a diagonal pattern. For a chevron the stitches would work four positions down and then four up as top right. Diamond and diaper patterns are evolved counting as for darning. The central area of silk (filoselle) is worked in the same way in tones of purple bronze lavender mixed with gold, and continued in soft lines to the base. Lines of crinkle pearl purl add a change of texture. It is amazing to remember that entire grounds of copes were worked in this method, with emblems and figures in split stitch. An example of this can be seen in the Syon Cope (Victoria and Albert Museum, London). The gold thread used then was a fine wire similar to fuse wire. The back shows the silk working thread and the minute loop of metal thread or silk drawn to the back

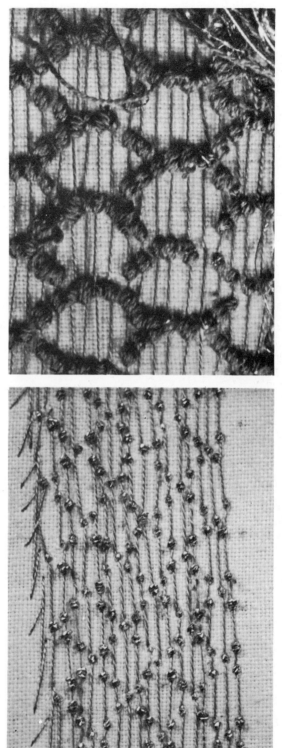

275–276 Details of back of embroidery

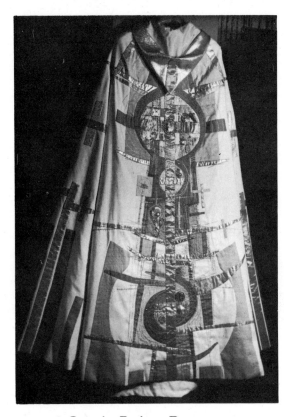
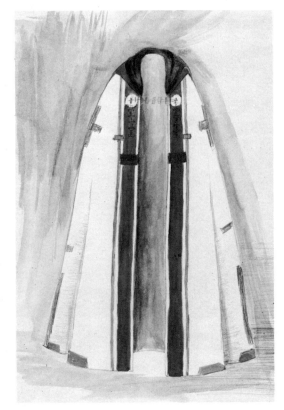

277, 278 Cope by Barbara Dawson

The design of the cope which aims to have dignity, simplicity, and richness and to reflect a feeling of space, has the main interest at the back to be seen by the congregation.

A central upright is crossed three times to make a trinity, and each cross is surrounded by a circle. The top cross is the most intricate, the next very simple and the third, at the hem, is freely composed, symbolising the freedom of present-day ideas, and is worked with least detail as it is least noticeable. The supporting shapes in the middle section are a concentrated arrangement of crosses and spheres.

The design is wider at the hem, than the top, and gold lines emanate from the centre in a circular manner giving an impression of the movement of a pendulum which fits the circular shape of the cope, and suggests a feeling of time and the enduring quality of faith.

The design is restrained at the sides but has rich and striking colour making a strong and Byzantine-like statement of a cross. The cloth of gold hood which surmounts the work at the back is repeated in the simple orphreys at the front, which show austere crosses.

The hem is united with the main design by appliqué in cloth of gold brilliant yellow and orange silk which makes radiating colour, and which serves a practical purpose as the applied pieces may be replaced if the hem shows signs of wear. The lining is a fine gold coloured cotton which is firm and helps to keep the cope in place when in use. The cope is darted at the shoulder for the same purpose.

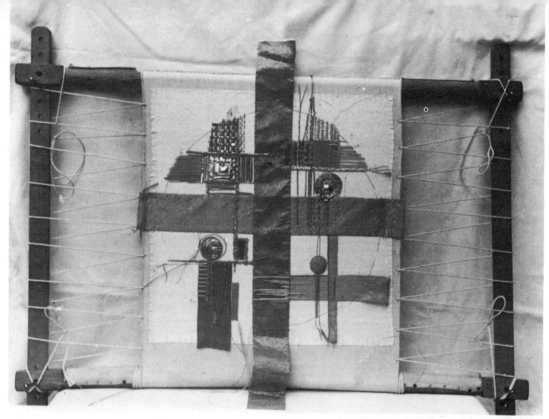

279–280 A backing of linen framed up with
extra material is rolled on the frame for padding if necessary. The cloth of gold is inter-
lined before being applied in position. The
circular surround is tacked out, and in each
segment a cross and a sphere is planned, with
silk appliqué laid work and padded shapes
prepared for gold thread

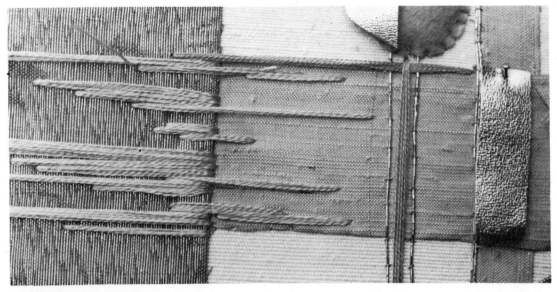

281 Detail of laid work

282 Detail of upper right. A padded area, couchingjapandpearlpurl,laidsilkandappliqué

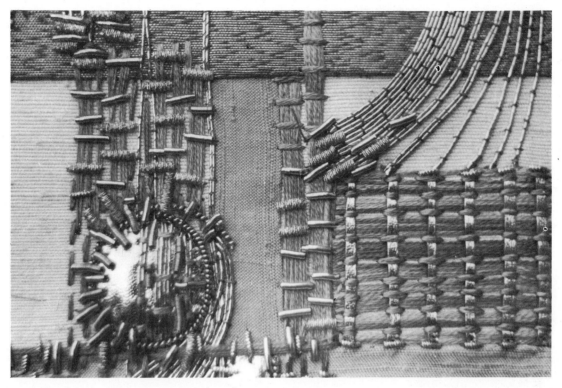

283 Circular lines from upper section. Lower circle completed, half in applied gold kid and the other half in rows of couched gold with the additional pattern of purl. Laid work in yellow and orange held in place by couched gold kid strips and purl.

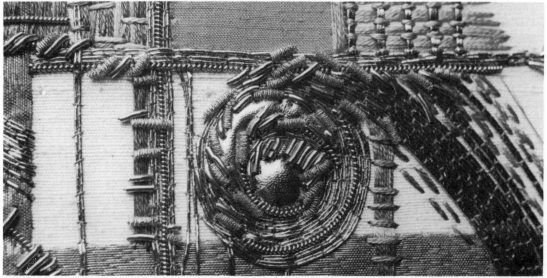

284 Detail of further stage at upper right, laid work held in place with purl, strips of kid couched in place with silk floss stitches. Padded circle completed with circulating couched lines flowing over bar of cross into lower segment. Laid work couched in fine pearl purl

285 Detail of centre

Opposite

286 Work on frame for assessment

287 With silk appliqué surround in position. The whirling lines in the paths of the orbs or spheres give a feeling of celestial space round the main cross

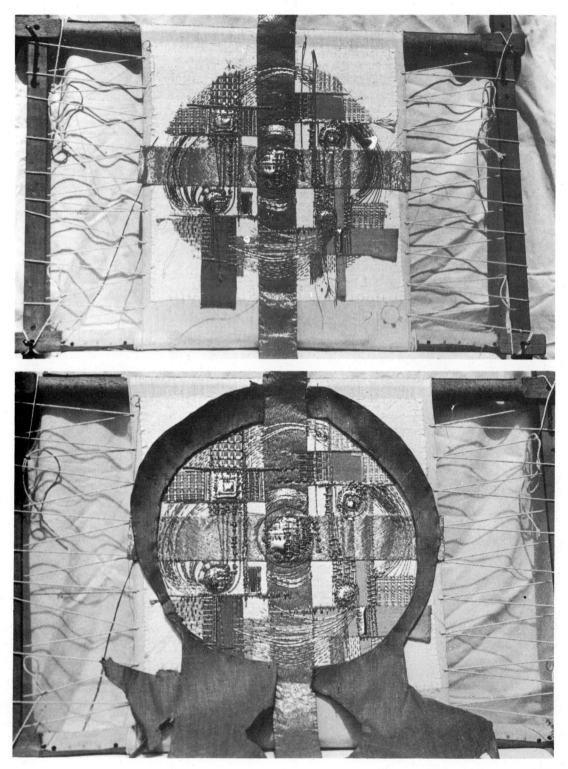

288, 289 Canons' copes which, with the Provost's cope, are part of a festal set of vestments commissioned by the Friends of Chelmsford Cathedral, for the Cathedral.

The Provost's cope has a design of spheres surrounding the cross richly arranged at the back, in contrast to the simple gold orphrey at the front. A silver morse accentuates the gold.

The Canons' copes are designed as a pair, the design being organised into a disciplined but decorative orphrey, in contrast to the plain orphrey of the Provost's cope, see figure 278. The colours of the orphreys are

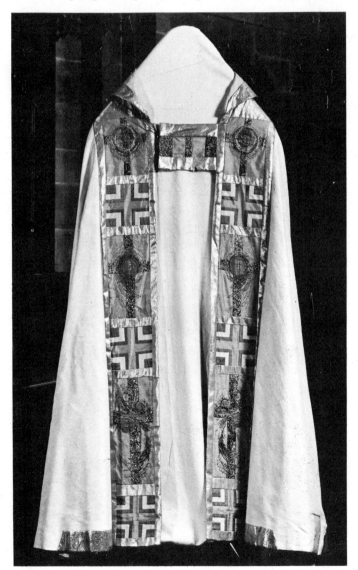

counterchanged, one cope having applied crosses in a dark coloured metal cloth on a light coloured silk, the other cope light coloured crosses on a dark silk background.

Split, stem and running stitch in floss silk are used to surround the appliqué and mark out the circles of the spheres.

The orphrey is made with alternating square sections worked in silk appliqué. The sections are joined together with strips of cloth of gold and then edged on each side in the same way

290 The third Canon's cope is further simplified and the floss embroidery is worked in the
smaller sections of the orphrey in a controlled
circle on an applied cross. The larger sections
are simple appliqué crosses in cloth of gold.
The material used is the same as on the simpler
Provost's cope

291 The back of all three copes are similarly
treated with stripes of different coloured silks
and golds used in the appliqué

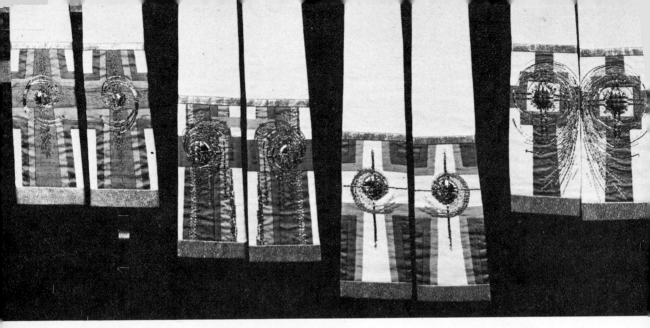

292 The four stoles of the festal set of vestments are each worked as a pair. If the design is not symmetrical, it is important to remember to reverse the design in order to avoid it facing the same way on both ends of the stole.

Each stole shows a cross and a sphere in appliqué, with gold thread and floss silk embroidery. In figure 1 the background is applied with silks as in the alternate sections of the orphreys, the cross is similar to the orphrey of the Provost's cope.

The decoration of the spheres is similar to that in the main circle of the design at the back of the Provost's cope. See page 186

293 Stoles
294 Detail

295 Shows the cross covering the seam at the back of the stole. This gives a guide to centre back in wear.

296 Detail of 297

297 Stole 3

298 The altar cross with the burse and veil.

The design of the burse repeats the idea from the orphrey of the Provost's cope, and the circle in the middle from the embroidery of the cope. The radiating lines in couched silk surrounding the cross take up the diagonal lines of the cross. The lines of couching are repeated in the veil round the cloth of gold cross. A small silk cross is worked onto the large cross to indicate the centre front when in use. The veil covers the chalice, which is one of the most precious parts of the communion, and, as many other precious objects, is given a special wrapping or covering

299 Detail of burse

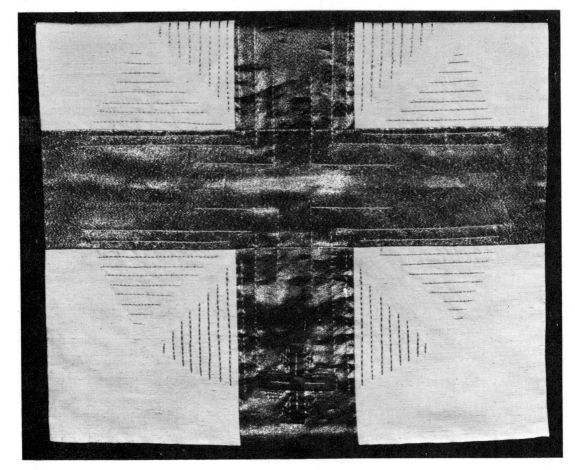

302 Altar frontal and altar hangings
The crosses at the side repeat the diagonal sections of the altar cross, and the centre cross carries the motif from the Provost's cope.

The hangings are decorated with coloured stripes of cloth of gold and silk as in the orphreys and decoration at the back of the Canons' copes

303 Detail of circle surrounding central cross

A design for a burse, either for Lent or Ascension, based on a simplified human figure with arm uplifted in either joy or anguish

304 The figure is worked on a rich red silk background in couched jap gold and couched floss silks in strong pink, red and blue.

Interest occurs in the change of light on the rows of gold which fill in the figure.

The area surrounding the figure is marked out as a grid in couched gold and is filled in with blocks of satin stitch in brilliant jewel colours of blue, purple, red, green, and yellow floss silk, in the manner of early enamel work.

The supporting figures of praise at each side are worked in purls over felt padding

Barbara Dawson

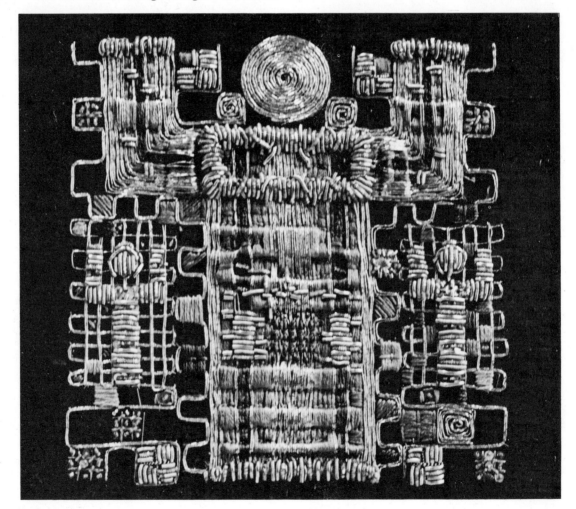

206

305 A design developed from the unit of the
figure

306 The figure is worked on blue and magenta shot silk handwoven in Wales. Burden stitch in jap gold is embroidered in floss silks of blue and magenta and yellow. Gold purls are sewn down in the same system as for the silks and are worked into a pattern to give a raised texture for the figure and for the mourning figures at the side.

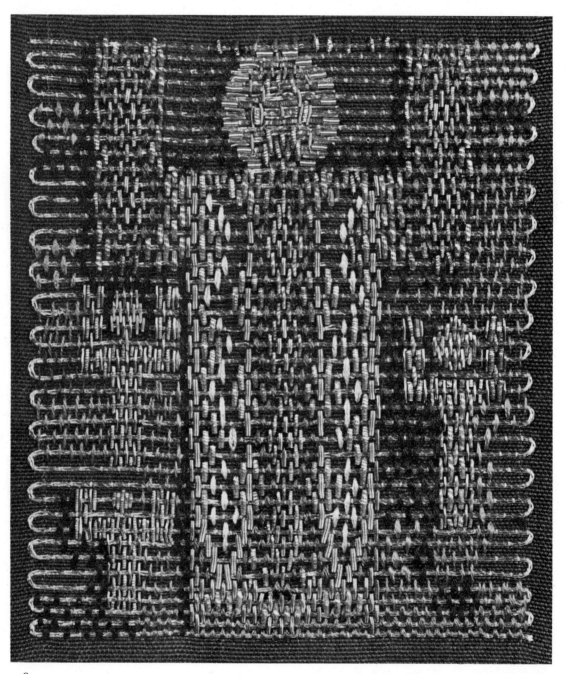

307 Burse *St Luke*. Dark olive green furnishing fabric, couched gold passing and crinkle thread, large and small pearl purl, with padded circle in different gold purls forming a cross *Susan Gaskell*

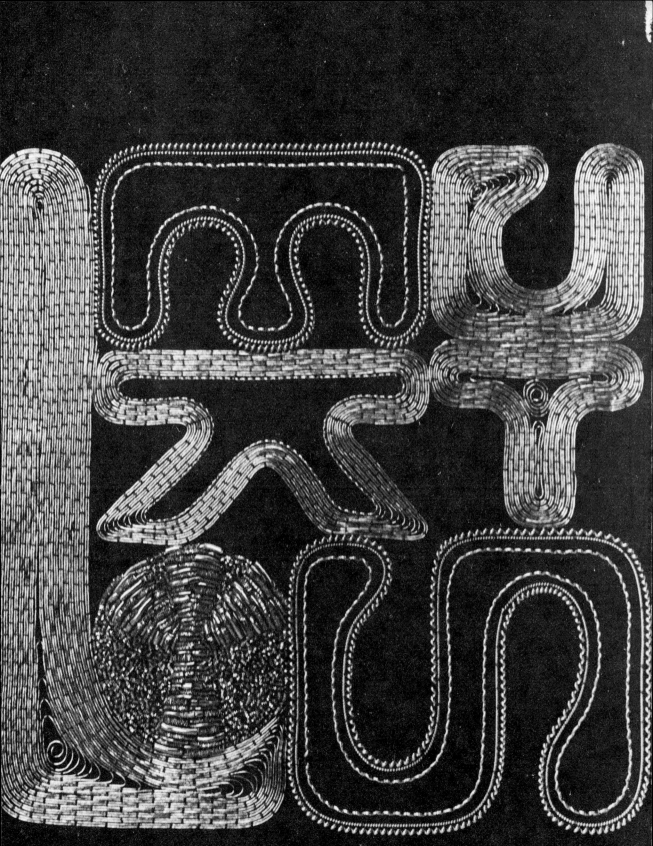

Bibliography

Inspiration for Embroidery
Constance Howard, Batsford London and
Branford Newton Centre, Massachusetts

Ecclesiastical Embroidery (out of print)
Beryl Dean, Batsford London and
Branford Newton Centre, Massachusetts

Ideas for Church Embroidery
Beryl Dean, Batsford London and
Branford Newton Centre, Massachusetts

Basic Design: The Dynamics of Visual form
Maurice de Saumarez, Studio Vista

Creative Drawing: Point and Line
Ernst Röttger and Dieter Klaute, Batsford London and
Reinhold New York

The Painter of Modern Life
Essays by Charles Baudelaire, Phaidon London

Rembrandt, Life and Work
Jakob Rosenberg, Phaidon London

Gold: Its Beauty, Power and Allure
C. H. V. Sutherland, Thames and Hudson London

The Art of Colour
Johannes Itten, Reinhold New York 1962

Motif 8 & 9
Shenval Press London

Machine Embroidery
Christine Risley, Studio Vista London

Embroidery and Collage
Eirian Short, Pitman (Matisse Vestments)

Church Vestments
Nora Jones, Embroiders Guild London

Principles of Pattern
Richard M. Proctor
Van Nostrand Reinhold, New York

Suppliers

Metal threads, braids and spangles
Mary Allen, Turnditch, Derbyshire.
Art Needlework Industries Ltd, 7 St Michael's Mansions, Ship Street, Oxford.
Louis Grossé Ltd, 36 Manchester Street, London W.1. (Substitute jap gold).
Mace and Nairn, 89 Crane Street, Salisbury, Wiltshire.
A. R. Mowbray & Company Ltd, 28 Margaret Street, London W.1.
The Needlewoman Shop, Regent Street, London W.1.
Christine Riley, 53 Barclay Street, Stonehaven, Cincardineshire.
Royal School of Needlework, 25 Princes Gate, London S.W.7.
Toye Kenning and Spencer Limited, Regalia House, 26 Red Lion Square, London W.C.1.
Elizabeth Tracy, Pathfield House, 45 High Street, Haslemere, Surrey.
Watts and Company Limited, 7 Tufton Street, London S.W.1.
J. Wippell and Company Limited, 11 Tufton Street, London S.W.1,
    55–56 High Street, Exeter, Cathedral Yard, Exeter and 24–26 King Street, Manchester.
The House of Vanheems, 47 Berners Street, London W.1.

Maltese Silk as above

Soutache braid
Soie, 13 Charlotte Street, London W.1.

D.M.C. (French) Threads particularly machine gold and silver synthetic threads and ordinary machine
sewing threads, tapestry and crewel wools
M.R., 1a Thornford Road, Lewisham, London S.E.13.
Braids (Soutache) Dorures Louis Mathieu, 130 Rue Raeumur, Paris 2e, France.

Jewels
Ells and Farrier, 5 Princes Street, Hanover Square, London W.1.

Leather gold and silver kid and other pliable leathers
The Light Leather Company, 16 Soho Square, London W.1.

Ground materials To explore personal choice in the furnishing and dress textile departments of:
Liberty and Company Limited, Regent Street, London W.1.
Peter Jones, Sloane Square, London S.W.1.
Heal and Son Limited, 196 Tottenham Court Road, London W.1.
John Lewis and Company Limited, Oxford Street, London W.1.
Harrods Limited, Brompton Road, London S.W.1.

Welsh flannel
Rural Industries Bureau, Wimbledon Common, London S.W.15.

Linen scrim
Dicksons and Company (Dungannon) Limited, Dungannon, Co. Tyrone, N. Ireland.

Natural and white linen, backings including old bleach linen
Mary Allen, Turnditch, Derbyshire.
The Needlewoman Shop, Regent Street, London W.1.
Harrods Limited, Brompton Road, London S.W.1.
Mace and Nairn, 89 Crane Street, Salisbury, Wilts.

Interlinings, bumph, cambric, lining and beeswax
Peter Jones, Sloane Square, London S.W.1.
John Lewis and Company Limited, Oxford Street, London W.1.
MacCullough and Wallis Limited, 25 Dering Street, London W.1.

General equipment, embroidery threads, needles and beeswax
The Needlewoman Shop, Regent Street, London W.1.
Harrods Limited, Brompton Road, London W.1.
John Lewis and Company Limited, Oxford Street, London W.1.
Mace and Nairn, 89 Crane Street, Salisbury, Wilts.

Suppliers in the USA
Aerolyn Fabrics Incorporated, 380 Broadway (Corner of White Street), New York, New York.
Bucky King Embroideries Unlimited, 121 South Drive, Pittsburgh, Pennsylvania 15238.
Macey's, Fifth Avenue, New York, New York.
The Needles' Point Studio, 7013 Duncraig Court, Mc Lean, Virginia 22101.
The Rusty Needle, 1479 Glenneyre, Laguna Beach, California 92651.
Tinsel Trading Company, 7 West 36th Street, New York 18, New York.

Embroidery threads and accessories
Appleton Brothers of London, West Main Road, Little Compton, Rhode Island 02837
American Thread Corporation, 90 Park Avenue, New York, N.Y. 10016
Bucky King Embroideries Unlimited, 121 South Drive, Pittsburgh, Pa. 15238
Craft Yarns, P.O. Box 35, Pawtucket, Rhode Island 02862
Lily Mills, Shelby, North Carolina 28150
The Sun Shop, 7722 Maple Street, New Orleans, La. 70118
The Makings, 1916 University Avenue, Berkeley, California 95704

Index

The numbers in *italics* refer to illustrations